GW01315769

*In a country where gender-based violence (GBV) has become normalised, GBV victims are gripped into believing that they are at fault and that their behaviour attracts the abuse. They are further shamed into carrying the burden of preventing abuse through 'identifying the red flags' and 'walking away', with the weight never on the abuser. Between these pages, Vanessa walks you through the darkest patches of her life as she witnessed her body and soul crushed at the hands of an abuser. This is her voice, one that will trigger and unearth many wounds while ushering a breath of healing to many women; silent or not.*

– Malebo Sephodi, academic and author of
bestselling book *Miss Behave*

*When a cut heals, the scar lies that the suffering is over. In this poignant account, Vanessa finds the courage to turn herself inside out, to show her deep wounds and to 'tell'. It's a story of family, of loyalty, of love and of betrayal. But, ultimately, it's a story of self-love, earned experience by experience, and the incremental gathering of strength.*

– Iman Rappetti, author of bestselling book *Becoming Iman*

*It is incredible how far off the mark our perception of people can be, particularly people with a high public profile. Vanessa and I were colleagues for a very brief period when eNCA was launched, but she pretty much kept to herself in those early days and was a bit of an enigma. Like most South Africans, I was only really acquainted to her through her work as a reporter. And it was in that role that she was in her element, exuding confidence, but little did I know that beneath that glamorous veneer, a tortured soul lay hidden.*

*This book is a brutally honest account of what I can only imagine was a living hell. Page after page I read in absolute horror of the brutality she endured at the hands of someone who 'loved' her. The sheer violence of the beatings she describes would flatten most men, let alone what I recall to be her petite figure.*

*I kept reading, waiting for this monster to be unmasked. Who was this evil bastard? Who is this cruel man? Actually, he is no grotesque figure from a Hollywood film – instead he is your brother, your boss, your doctor, your colleague, and therefore it could even be me. The grim statistics will tell you that he is your typical South African man. But ultimately it doesn't really matter who he is. This is not his story. This is the story of another heroic survivor of a deeply prevalent, but unspoken, South African secret. And what a story it is!*
*– THABISO TEMA, EDITOR OF DESTINY MAN*

# Beaten
*but not* **Broken**

# *Beaten* but not *Broken*

Vanessa Govender

Published by Jacana Media (Pty) Ltd
First, second and third impression 2018

10 Orange Street
Sunnyside
Auckland Park 2092
South Africa
+2711 628 3200
www.jacana.co.za

© Vanessa Govender, 2018

Cover photo courtesy of Sean Baker photography

The author has tried to recreate events, locales and conversations from her memories of them. In order to maintain their anonymity and privacy, the names of individuals and places have been withheld or altered in some instances.

All rights reserved.

ISBN 978-1-4314-2679-9

Cover design by Palesa Motsomi
Editing by Joey Kok
Proofreading by Lara Jacob
Set in Minion Pro 11/16.5pt
Printed and bound by CTP Printers, Cape Town
Job no. 003430

See a complete list of Jacana titles at www.jacana.co.za

*For Dad and for David*
*If the greatness of a man is to be measured by what he evokes and instils in those around him, even long after he is gone, his legacy lingers on, then you both remain the greatest men I will ever know.*

*In memory of the thousands of women who never made it out alive.*

*In honour of the thousands more who are looking for a way out.*
*You are courageous beyond your own comprehension.*
*Come, take my hand and walk a while with me.*

# *Foreword*

Ifirst met Vanessa Govender when she joined eNCA as a rookie reporter on the cusp of fame. I thought at the time that she was a smart, driven, talented, care-free young woman with the world at her feet. What I did not know was that she was battling horrific domestic violence – abuse she regarded as a shameful, dirty secret believing that she was somehow responsible for it. Here was I – a seasoned investigative journalist – with absolutely no idea that Vanessa was coming to work every day with bruises smashed into her body and her soul.

Sadly, there are far too many Vanessas waking up every day, putting on make-up to hide the beatings and a brave face to mask the pain.

*Beaten but not Broken* is a harrowing read – it is hard enough to read about domestic violence, harder still when you know the person involved. Her story is not new – there are thousands more with similar tales in South Africa – but it is told with a searing honesty that at times makes you want to flinch and turn away.

But please don't look away! One of the ways we can do justice to Vanessa's story is by reading it, by walking with her as she recounts her torment. What is compelling about her book is that it is written by someone who is famous and beautiful, and on the surface seems to 'have it all'. It is a cruel reminder that domestic abuse is not about race, wealth, position or education; it can and does happen to anyone. It is that awful taboo kept hidden in the dark and dusty corners of our society because women are too scared or too ashamed to speak out. Vanessa suffered a double injustice – she had to fight to break free of her abuser and then she had to fight the debilitating shame that slowly snaked its way through her, eating away at her confidence and self-respect.

The #MeToo Movement has resulted in a seismic shift for women. Whereas previously we fought simply to be taken seriously on the issue of sexual harassment and domestic violence, now not only are these stories believed but there are consequences, with powerful men starting to fall.

Yet, the bitter truth is that more than two decades into our democracy, South Africa is still known as the rape capital of the world. We have learnt to live with terrifying statistics – one in three women will be raped in our lifetime, every 26 seconds a woman is raped in this country. More often than not, her rapist is someone she knows or her most intimate partner.

Read this book and weep for all those women who have suffered and often died at the hands of their abusers.

But read it too and feel empowered.

It is not too late to speak out if you are in an abusive relationship or know someone who is in abusive relationship.

And it is never too late to teach our sons that no *always* means no, and if they are not sure it's a no – to ask again.

That being strong is not about how hard you hit or how much force you exert over a woman.

And that using a woman as a punching bag for your own rage and insecurity is the work of a coward not a real man – her body does not belong to you.

It has been said far too often that the only way to break this cycle of violence is for women to speak out. And yet sometimes speaking out is even harder than bearing the abuse – the worst lies are the ones we tell to protect ourselves. It is our silence and our squeamishness about domestic violence that hurts everyone involved.

Vanessa has found the courage to share her ordeal in the hope that it will inspire others to find their voice. We owe her the dignity of reading her story, seeing her pain, saluting her bravery and creating a space for other abused women to know they can step out of the shadows and end the silence. It doesn't matter if it's a quiet whisper or a deafening roar – the time to listen empathically and fight fiercely to end it is NOW.

Debora Patta

# ONE

## *Endings and Beginnings*

Every story has a beginning. Mine starts at the end.

So many voices, all talking at the same time, all rushing at me. I could hear my father's voice among them. I couldn't quite decipher what he was saying. I couldn't make sense of what any of those disembodied voices were saying. All of them tangled together inside my head talking urgently, talking over each other.

Voices in the darkness, hollow and distant.

Who these voices belonged to I had no idea.

There was no mistaking my father's voice though.

It was comforting, but it was freaking me out.

My father was dead! Why was he talking to me? How could he be talking to me? Did this mean I was dead too?

That realisation hit me as hard as the loud symphony of voices inside my aching head.

My father, Frank, had been dead for more than a year. But I could hear him as clear as day. He couldn't be dead after all. I must have dreamt that.

I tried to sift out individual voices to try and make sense of what they were saying to me. I tried to focus on just one voice.

But I couldn't. I was struggling, trapped inside my own head, trying to claw my way out. Those voices, as jarring and as jumbled as they all were – without faces – coaxed me out of the darkness that I didn't even know I had slipped into.

Softly enticing me out of the dead, cold place inside my brain, lifting me out of the blackness that filled my head.

I gasped greedily for air. It felt like I hadn't had any for an eternity. Suddenly I was awake, alert!

Had I stopped breathing? Was I trapped in that space somewhere between life and death? I could feel nothing. I had been stuck in some hollow place that was barren, without colour, without life. It was empty, save for the faceless voices that came at me from every direction. There was nothing inside my head.

Close your eyes, and there will always be images flickering, memories flitting by. But there was nothing inside my head, just the never-ending blackness. It was thick and suffocating.

I don't know if my life tried to escape from the physical place that my body was in. I blinked my eyes open. Nothing I saw made any sense. I was lying face down in the SABC parking lot.

People talk of near-death experiences. I think that evening I had one of my own. I felt claustrophobic in that wide-open space.

I could feel panic wash over me, and I wanted to scream.

I don't know how long I had been out for. A few minutes or a few seconds? It seemed like it had been forever. What happened? How did I end up there?

My eyes fought back the tears that threatened an avalanche. I'm not sure why or how, but I just knew that crying at that moment would seem pathetic. The sobs stayed stuck in my throat, and fear seeped out of every pore and into the cold, hard, unfeeling concrete beneath me, punishing me for my poor choices.

It took some time for my eyes to adjust to the fading daylight.

I could feel the cold and damp penetrating my clothes and reaching into my skin.

I began to shiver, more from fear than from the chill of that winter's evening in Durban. Funny how the memory stores what can seem like the most inane of details in a time of trauma.

Bit by bit I started to make sense of my surroundings, the blackness inside my head begrudgingly making way for consciousness.

Slowly I was making sense of myself. I had a pounding headache. My nose stung, and my face felt like it was on fire. I could taste blood.

And just as everything seemed to unfold in slow motion, it all suddenly began to come together fast. Still lying on the ground, I turned my head and looked straight into a pair of shoes. I smelled his cigarette smoke. I couldn't breathe. So much air around me, yet I felt like I was suffocating.

I close my eyes now, more than a decade later, and I am back there on that floor.

I can feel all of it, like an out-of-body experience. I need to go back there and to so many other places, so that I can truly move forward to where I am now, so that I can be present in the here and now. But to be present in the here and now, I must take a few steps back.

The time has come to speak my truth. It has been waiting patiently, biding its time inside my head. My truth, dusty with lies and scattered in my memory.

With a lot of effort, I pushed myself up. My body ached. Every movement required mental coercion, my mind coaxing my limbs.

I stood, a little unsteady on my feet, and looked at him, searching his face for answers. He didn't even have to say a word. A horrified look swept over his face as he drank in the damage. His unreadable, passive face changed within seconds.

Under different circumstances, I might have had a good chuckle at the swift change of expression. Except there was nothing remotely funny about the disaster my own face had become. But for those few seconds, while I stood before him, I remained blissfully unaware of the extent of the damage, of just how horribly my face had morphed into something utterly unsightly while my brain shut down and took me to that place of blackness.

He sucked on that cigarette like his life depended on it. I knew the signs all too well. His body language read like a cheap and predictable story. He was agitated. It was stress, it was fear, and his calculating brain was in overdrive. I could see it. I could smell it, and I could even hear him thinking above the sounds of the chirruping crickets and whooshing cars on the nearby road. Oh, I knew him well! Better than he probably knew himself.

And in that instant came the realisation – it was like being awakened roughly from a deep sleep – of the horror that had happened to me.

I could tell he had a story ready for me. I think he was talking. I saw his mouth moving. I wasn't hearing. I couldn't hear. I couldn't hear above the anger, the rage, the fear and the hate that overflowed from my head and heart.

I walked to his car, my unsteady feet catching in my long denim skirt, my heart thumping furiously in my chest, in my ears. Could he hear it?

I lowered myself into the passenger seat of his BMW, every movement a shockwave of pain. He had followed me. Now I heard his whiney voice – no breaks, no pauses, it was just this monotonous vomit-inducing sound that assaulted my ears – but I was not listening to him.

There was no space outside my head and heart for my anger and fear. I knew it had to be kept hidden at all costs. You just know these things.

You know there is never any room on the outside for what is raging on the inside.

I switched on the car's interior light and looked in the tiny mirror. Nothing though could have prepared me for what I saw. My forehead was swollen; it was bulging, angry and misshapen. The skin on my nose and chin had been completely ripped off. It was red, and it was burning like hell, tiny pieces of dirt clinging to the raw bits of my face. The sight took my own breath away. I was unrecognisable. Dear God, I looked hideous. I looked nothing like myself. A scream stayed stuck in my throat.

I couldn't believe my eyes. I never thought myself particularly pretty before, but I was struck by how utterly ugly I suddenly was.

He was kneeling at the car door, still puffing on the dregs of his cigarette. Or had he lit another one? The stench of brandy hung on his warm breath. It travelled the small space between us. It washed over my face, entered my nose and made my stomach churn.

Instead of turning away, as always, I looked at him, searching his eyes, his face for the truth.

I was never beyond allowing him the opportunity for redemption. All it would have taken was seeing actual regret and sorrow in his eyes. His words meant nothing. It was always his eyes I searched to know if there was any truth to his words.

In all the years we were together, in all those times of violence, I never, not once ever, saw remorse or sorrow in his eyes. He said the right words, but the, 'I am sorry, I didn't mean to do it, forgive me' – the deep regret of those forlorn words never actually reached his eyes.

'What have you done?' my voice bitter, bile rising to my mouth. Hatred coursed through my veins like acid, polluting my senses, filling my head.

But I had to play my cards right. I couldn't get confrontational. 'I must not argue,' I told myself. I must not start a fight. My body and my brain defeated but still knowing the rules of engagement and how to play this game to ensure my safety.

I had fallen, he said. We were talking, and I had just suddenly fallen to the ground.

I wanted to laugh. Really? I just fell to the ground?

I knew in my deepest of hearts I didn't just fall to the ground like he said. The injuries I had involved brute force. Did he throw me against the car door? Or did he slam my face into the ground? I don't know. I would never know because the only person who had the answers was never going to reveal what had happened.

I looked into his black eyes, noticing for the first time how close-set they were, making him look utterly repugnant. At that moment, though, they were also empty and couldn't focus, thanks to the booze. Anger fuelled with copious amounts of brandy was a bad combination. Alcohol always turned him bellicose, even more so than he was in his sober state, and that's saying something.

I saw fear creeping in and nesting quietly in the corners of those cold black eyes. Because this time there would be no hiding the evidence, even if I tried. He'd left scars and bruises before, but they were easy to hide. A little make-up or clever story, and no one really bothered to delve deeper or question what they were seeing and being told. But this time there was no way I'd be able to hide behind make-up, and there was no plausible story that even I, a storyteller by profession, could come up with to explain these injuries. I think he realised that his pernicious handiwork was going to expose him for who and what he really was. He was afraid for himself. He went through great lengths to create the image of the consummate professional, the virtuous boyfriend – charming, debonair, every step, every word carefully chosen to portray himself as perfection personified – and now all of that could collapse catastrophically and ruin his career and him. The risk of the real him – the him that I knew – now being exposed for all to see was there.

He took me home that night, even though he didn't want to. He was scared. All the way as he drove, he kept pestering me about what I was going to say to my mother. 'The truth,' I told him and remained silent for the rest of the journey.

I should have been afraid. He was drunk and desperate, but I didn't care. I was past caring. I just wanted to get home. I should have never gotten into the car with him when I really couldn't trust him, but I was past being afraid of him too. What more could he possibly do to me? I was exhausted, acutely aware of how utterly empty I felt. I felt nothing, absolutely nothing. Even my simmering rage had subsided. A place like that can be dangerous, or it can be liberating. It can drive you to do something crazy or it can simply steer you out to make a change.

It is a strange place to be, unafraid and in the midst of danger. I knew the propensity for violence of the person sitting next to me; I was within his reach, yet I was so out of touch with myself that I didn't even care.

He kept insisting he didn't do this to me, that I must believe that he would never do something like this.

He said it was my fault. Now that was a line I had heard a thousand times before.

I had fallen, he kept repeating.

I sat silently in the car, staring out of the window, my head and body aching. Feeling desperately sad. Worn out and done! It wasn't even a conscious thought. It was just there in my head and heart, consoling almost. I wanted out. I needed out. It was over. Even though I didn't quite know it at the time.

This was to be the last time he would ever lay a hand on me. This violent ending would be the start of a whole new life.

It was late when I got home, and I didn't have an explanation. No sooner had I even stepped out of his car and I was already planning to lie for him again. But I have never lied for *him*. No, survivors of abuse never lie for their abusers. It's what we tell ourselves, that we want to protect the men we supposedly love.

The truth is we lie to protect *ourselves*. No one must know who we really are. That beneath the smiles and laughs we carefully and calculatingly display, to charm those around us and make them ignore their niggling feeling that something isn't quite right, beneath all of that is just a frightened, defeated, barely existing, pathetic little victim.

Like our abusers, we are also masters of deception. We can fool you into thinking we're loved, in love and content. From the very first time we are struck, we just know how to deceive.

I let myself into the house. It was just my mom, Neela, and I living there. My two sisters, Rita and Preshene, had married and moved out. My father was dead and gone. The silence of a once-full home rang in my ears.

I was desperate to clean myself. But there was no way I could manage lowering myself into the bathtub in the bathroom I used. My body ached too much. So I quietly slipped into my mother's en suite bathroom; she had a shower. Standing up would be far easier for my battered and bruised body. Despite my careful attempts to be quiet, my mother woke up, asking me how I was doing from the darkness of her room.

'Good!' I called out, nothing in my voice to give away the trauma and the anguish that coursed through me. All I wanted to do was cry, cry and never stop crying.

Hot water ran down the length of my body, as I stood rooted to one spot. I gently ran a bar of soap under my arms, down my legs. I had to bite back moaning as I attempted to wash my face. I just had to remove my make-up. Everyone knows you can't go to bed with make-up on – it ages you. Carefully avoiding soap getting onto my raw nose and chin, I gingerly used my fingertips to wash the parts of my face that escaped injury. The hot water seared my raw skin. Water punishing me for betraying myself yet again. But I wasn't going to bed with make-up on.

Self-control was key. My mother asked me to turn on the light when I made my way back into her bedroom.

'What for?' I barked. She said that she just wanted to see me, that she hadn't seen me all day. Was it mother's intuition? There was never getting anything past my mom, as the coming hours would show.

I snapped at her: 'It's late. Please. Don't annoy me. I don't have time for this. I want to sleep.'

I curled up beside my mother, turning my back on her just in case the soft light shining in from outside the bedroom window would reveal my injuries.

I was desperate to be held by safe arms. To feel safe hands touch me. My body ached from so much more than the physical pain. It ached for comfort. But for now, lying curled up next to my mom would have to do. I needed the closeness of a safe person.

I had a 5am call time the following day and was out of the house before my mother could wake up. I had stolen a few more hours to concoct a colossal lie.

It was June 2005. I was a month into my new job as a television news reporter at e.tv. That morning we were covering a taxi strike in Inanda just outside Durban.

I walked through the doors of the e.tv office in Greyville, a few hundred metres from the SABC studios where I was just the night before. My head filled with a thousand thoughts. What was I going to say to my colleagues? How was I going to explain?

Sibusiso Miya, the camera operator assigned to work with me on the story, was already getting the equipment ready. He turned to greet me, but his warm smile immediately turned into a look of absolute shock when he saw my face. I saw pity in his eyes and could tell instantly that he was intuitive and would listen and only pretend to laugh when I was nonchalantly trying to explain away my bumps and bruises.

I wasn't mentally prepared to see the look of pity I saw in his eyes that morning. Sbu later told me that by that time he'd already heard the rumours about me that were circulating in Durban's media circles. Journalists, photographers, they'd all been talking. People had suspected, but they never let on what they thought they knew.

I wanted to put a paper bag over my face. It hurt to have him look at me. I felt so conspicuous, ugly and dirty. I wanted to cry again. I felt utterly spent and desperate. But I was deeply ensnared in my own trap of lies and sorrow. More than the actual knowledge of being an abused woman and victim, the thing that made me feel incredibly sad and lonely was the look of pity in the eyes of people around me, colleagues and strangers alike. Like they could read the story of the fresh bruises that every so often would dent my face.

Do you know what that's like? People almost want to steer clear of you when they notice your injuries, like you have something contagious. As soon as your eyes meet theirs, they quickly look away. They don't want to see you. They wish they hadn't seen you. How can they un-see what they've just seen? That's how I felt every single time someone looked at me, their eyes skimming over my bruises and scars, taking it all in before quickly looking away. Sometimes I got a smile. Not a full, happy one, but a fleeting, sad smile that cut to the core, making me feel even more pathetic than I already knew I was. I'm quite sure I wasn't imagining it. Or maybe it was all in my head, nothing more than a deep, desperate desire for empathy. A visceral need to just be seen.

It's almost like what some of us do when confronted by beggars. If we look away quickly enough, they don't exist. We don't see their anguish, their struggle.

My shameful, pathetic story was always so transparent on my face.

For more than 2000 days I wore my humiliation like a second skin and carried my dark secret, a permanent piece of baggage, heavy and laden with deceit; a piece of baggage that I could never put down. I was cursed to carry it wherever I went.

This time was no different.

I managed to give Sbu a bright and cheery smile, but it made my face ache.

I had a head full of scheming stories and a mouth full of lies. The story I would tell began to take shape as soon as I walked into the e.tv office that morning, and Sbu would be the first person I would test it out on. If I could convince him, then I could convince everybody else.

'I was running,' I told him, 'and I was wearing a long skirt, and I tripped and fell.' Small little bits of truth immersed in the deception. Carefully woven together, so that no one could sift out what was true and what wasn't.

There it came. In an instant, as I opened my mouth, the story told itself. The lovely little lie had unfolded. I even managed a bashful smile, or at least I attempted what I hoped was a bashful smile.

My forehead was bulging, and the thick layer of foundation and face powder caked on the raw skin on my nose, doing nothing to hide the scars. I'm not sure if I looked more crazy than bashful. But you can't blame a girl for trying. Even abused women want to look pretty. Although not too pretty, as we can't be seen to be making too much of an effort, lest we incur the spite and wrath of our abusers.

Sbu looked like he didn't believe me. He looked sad, which made me feel like I could just tell him the truth. We barely knew each other. How could a stranger feel pity for me? And was my lie so transparent that someone I didn't know could see it for what it was? Could he see me for what I was?

How I wished in that instant I could just speak the truth. Let it all tumble out. But would anyone else want to hear it when I myself struggled to accept it?

Plus, the last thing I wanted to do was label myself as a victim.

Certainly not when I just started a new job – a very public profile job. e.tv was only really in its infancy stages when I joined, but its daily prime-time news was fast gaining momentum. At the height of my career at e.tv, between 2009 and 2011, the half hour news bulletin would attract more than one million viewers.

That's over one million people who knew my name and my face. From South Africa's poorest communities to the most affluent of suburbs, from car guards to CEOs and politicians – people whom I didn't know knew me. Or they thought they did. I was Vanessa Govender, journalist and television news reporter. People admired me. I heard the wonder in their voices and saw the awe in their eyes. I'd get stopped in public. People wanted to take photos or just chat with me. I'd be inundated with messages on social media.

Seductive and addictive, fame was a drug, every bit as intoxicating as it was lethal. And when you've clawed your way out from the depths of the hell you've experienced at the hands of another human being, fame can fix you – and it can also turn you a little into an unassuming savage leaching off praise. I greedily gathered the affection and adoration of strangers, men and women and children.

I'd go out and expect to be recognised, and I was never disappointed. Fame found me, and I turned fame into a slave that fed my insatiable desire never wanting to be unseen and unknown. Fame ameliorated my broken spirit, my dying self-esteem.

Fame was delicious. I swallowed, no, gulped the praise and admiration down greedily. I was always hungry for more. I could never get enough. For so long I had been in the shadows, as the girlfriend of a popular radio DJ who hardly acknowledged me as such in public, and also as the Lotus FM newsreader who never quite made it. And now here I was, suddenly feeling seen and heard in the superficial spotlight that television casts.

How on earth could I be a victim? No, that part of me would be buried and forgotten about. I was in a new role now – a small-screen celebrity. There was no room to be a victim. There was no space for the sadness and hollowness that dogged me during my days at the SABC with him. No one must know of my terrible past and my shameful secret. How pathetic. It didn't go with the image. It certainly wouldn't add to my appeal. I had to portray the image of a strong woman. An 'ice princess', as one of my superiors once described me, aloof and unreadable. That's who everyone thought me to be. And that is exactly what I was going to be. I was going to be that strong, funny and happy girl that people admired. I was also going to be quiet and contemplative. I was all of this. And yet I was none of it too. No one would ever know that though. No one would know that once all the layers were peeled away, I was just a victim. I was nothing more than a girl with a terrible, shameful secret. I was a battered woman. I was one of many thousands of women in South Africa who got slapped and punched and kicked.

But I was not going to admit to being one of thousands, certainly not to the millions who watched me on television. No, that was my secret to keep, my truth to lie about.

To the country, to my family, to my friends and even to strangers I wasn't going to relinquish their perceptions of me. Not for one second. Their perceptions were far more attractive, far sexier and far more palatable than the reality, which could be summed up in just one little word: victim.

As I was battered and bruised, going out on a story that day was gruelling. I was surrounded by police officers, many of them eager to chat to the girl from TV. I tried to remain hidden, in the background, away from prying eyes. I sat in the car for most of that story. I would have done anything to not have to show my face. A reporter needs to be there in the thick of things, but how could I with the evidence of my shameful secret for all to see?

I had to call my editor, Patrick Conroy, and tell him I couldn't go on camera. In the coming months and years, I would come to relish and revel in the fact that my face flashed across millions of television screens across the country almost every night. It would be the unspoken declaration of my emancipation to and from him and anyone else who knew us together as a couple – my declaration that I was still standing.

But not that day. There was no way I could appear on television like that. I told Patrick that I'd fallen and injured my face. He laughed and said he wasn't even going to ask how. 'You wouldn't want to know anyway,' I said, laughing, relieved that I got off so easily, that I would not have to repeat the details of the whole despicable lie again.

My lie had fast entrenched itself in the office. The more I told the story, the more confident I became with it. In fact, I could even picture myself falling. I could visualise the whole scene.

My assumed clumsiness elicited laughs. In retrospect, the amusement of my new co-workers was uneasy. The humour never reached their eyes. But you see what you want to see. And I chose to see that I'd made them laugh.

When I got home, my mother was waiting for me at the door, something she never does. The last time she looked into my face was the morning before, when he had picked me up to spend my day off with him.

There was never any fooling my mother. There was no hiding now.

There was a sharp intake of breath when she saw me, and she clasped her hands around her cheeks. I'd seen this exaggerated, dramatic gesture so many times before and have come to lovingly understand it as characterising the stereotypical overprotective Indian mother. Except this time, the gesture was everything but exaggerated or dramatic – it was one made by a mother seeing the horribly disfigured face of her youngest child.

I started speaking before she could. Best to seize control of the situation before she did, I thought. 'I was covering a taxi strike at work,' I said. 'Things got a bit rough, and I got pushed during a confrontation between the police and taxi drivers.'

Another lie? Okay not so much, as the cops and protestors did sort of have a confrontation. But I observed from a safe distance, from the car.

Two different stories, two different lies.

There was disbelief in my mother's eyes. She kept asking if I was sure that's what happened, a barrage of questions in the face of my non-committal answers, and then she went quiet. I should have known though she would never leave it there.

He tried calling me several times that day and evening. I could sense the desperation in every ring of my cell phone. Ignoring his calls gave me a little bit of satisfaction. This time I was not afraid of the consequences.

I needed time, time to concoct the biggest lie that would ultimately save me and allow me to escape from him once and for all.

The next day, while I was out on another story, my mother called the office and quizzed Nicola Govender, the secretary, about what had happened. Shy and slightly eccentric, Nicola told her that I'd showed up at the office with the injuries, and as far as she knew, it didn't happen at the taxi strike, like I'd told my mother, but on my day off.

When I got back to the office, Nicola told me my mother had called to ask about my injuries. She sheepishly admitted what she'd told my mother. She was whispering, like she was complicit in the lie and understood something terrible had happened and was still happening. I laughed a little too loudly and told her my mom had probably misunderstood what I'd said but I would clear it up when I got home.

She persisted, 'I hope I haven't done anything wrong.'

'Don't stress … Really, it's all good,' I assured her.

She searched my face. I wished she would just go away.

On the drive home, I played out in my head what to tell my mother, how to fix this, smooth it over.

Word had reached Rita and Preshene thanks to my frantic mother's phone calls. My two sisters arrived at our family home, demanding answers. As they inspected my injuries, horror crept over their faces. All three demanded to know what happened. All of them were convinced he was responsible. They knew of his abusive streak.

I said if I'd told them that I had tripped and fell at the SABC, they would never have believed me, and thought he was responsible. So I lied to my mother, and told her it happened at the taxi strike. They weren't buying it. Rita rubbished my story. 'You don't get those kind of injuries from falling,' she said. Preshene was livid; the sight of my scarred face was more than she could bear. And she dragged my father into it: 'Your father never laid a hand on you, and you allow this scum to do this to you,' she said, accusingly. 'It's the truth!' I beseeched. But they never bought that story or my pleas to be believed.

I was protecting him again, but I couldn't tell anybody what really happened, because I didn't even know myself. All I knew was I couldn't account for the lost minutes (or was it seconds?) of my life before I woke up face down on a cold floor in a deserted parking lot. I couldn't say for certain how I ended up there. All I knew was what I believed in my heart to have happened. All I knew was what the injuries spoke of. All I knew was that violence and making up afterwards was all very much part of our crazy relationship.

A few days later one of the office security guards brought up a whole bunch of white balloons to the newsroom. Smiling knowingly, the gangly guard said a secret admirer had dropped them off. It was what he had been instructed to say. I had only been at e.tv for a month, and in that short space of time he had already befriended the security guards.

Befriending the guards was a strategic move. He also did it during my time at the SABC, and I suspect he paid them to tell him when and how I interacted, specifically with men around the office. It was uncanny how he knew so much about my movements and interactions when he was not with me, and I often wondered how he knew. When I saw him handing the guards a big black bag filled with some of his old clothes and a bottle of booze one day, the penny dropped. I realised the guards must have been feeding him information about me.

My scarred face turned hot with embarrassment as my colleagues teased me about a fan taking fancy to me.

And even though I'd wanted to believe their speculations, I'd received so many gifts from him over the years that I immediately knew from whom it was and what it signified. Only the security guard knew who gave me those balloons.

Why say sorry, I wondered. Why the peace offering when he was so adamant that he was not the cause of my injuries?

I let the whole bunch go before I stepped into my car and headed home that day, watched them lift into the air, and I was filled with hatred. Never had I despised anyone as much as I despised him.

Days turned into weeks, and I avoided seeing him. I avoided his calls. I punched in angry messages in answer to his SMS demands to see me again, the send button hit with force and contempt.

It was much easier to avoid him now that we were no longer working at the SABC together. There it was difficult not to run into him or walk out and see his car parked next to mine, with him waiting for me when I ignored him or did not respond to his calls after a fight. There was never any escaping. I was well and truly trapped, emotionally and physically.

For the first time in our five years and seven months together, he seemed to back off and go quiet after I rejected all his calls and text messages. Perhaps somewhere he also understood this thing between us was dying. Dead! Perhaps he finally clicked that he'd lost his hold on me.

I didn't know what it was at the time and couldn't even pinpoint where it came from, but I felt a surprising sense of release. I no longer had that overwhelming need for him. That weakness where my body and mind seemed to act independently of each other – and I'd end up back with him after a few days of wallowing, despite not really wanting to be with him – was waning. His apologies, tears and pleading that he loved me so much, that I drove him to it because he felt so intensely for me no longer meant anything. The words that thrilled me, gave me goose bumps and soothed me moments after suffering physical violence at his hands – those words no longer held me captive.

People talk of an 'a-ha' moment. That was mine. It was nothing dramatic. It was just a quiet sense of being done. Of heeding that feeling that coursed through me. It was finally acknowledging that I didn't love him and that I had never been in love with him.

'You don't need him,' said my inner voice. 'You never did. He said no one would love you like he did. But he doesn't love you. He never did. After you strip away the fancy clothes, the fancy car and the popularity, there's actually nothing much left of him to even like, never mind love.

'With him you're nothing, Vanessa. Without him, I dare say, you could do amazing things. You could leave an imprint that will remain long after you have gone.'

I wanted to live again. I wanted to breathe. I wanted to be happy and revel in it. I wanted to be who I was before I became the person I was with him.

The mind is a powerful thing. For a long time, I'd convinced myself I couldn't do better than him. I'd talked myself into staying because being alone was too terrible to contemplate. I told myself that the beatings were not that bad and that I was in large part to blame. I allowed myself to be convinced by what he told me. I allowed him to manipulate my mind and fill my head with subtle and cunning little words that gnawed at my self-esteem and whittled away my logic. I believed that if you were in a relationship for the long haul, you had to roll with the punches. Literally.

Once I allowed myself to do so, I was able to see a life without – and beyond – him. Once I'd given myself room to breathe and think, I was able to accept that being alone and single wasn't such a bad thing, and that I could do it and probably be happier on my own.

The same mind that kept me trapped, shackled and believing I could and would never do better than him was the one that eventually helped me break free from him, but only because I allowed it to.

The a-ha moment was a long time coming. It probably started with a request from e.tv's Aakash Bramdeo and McIntosh Nzimande (who later became McIntosh Polela) for me to take a screen test because I had the 'look' for TV. I was flattered to be asked to try out for a job on national television, and I secretly played Aakash's comment about my TV look over and over in my head. I greedily hung onto those words and revelled in them.

I was given about fifteen minutes to prepare for the screen test. I had to memorise a few lines that I would then need to present in front of the camera. It would be recorded and sent up to Johannesburg for e.tv's news bosses to look at. It was my first time in front of a television camera.

He was hovering in the background. He'd offered to drive me to the screen test. He said he wanted to come along just to see if I had what it took to make it on TV. I suspect he didn't think I would stand a chance.

It took me fewer than five minutes to learn the lines. It took me even less time to deliver it on camera. I think everyone – including me – was a little surprised that it took one take. No fluffing, no mistakes, just once, and it was done.

I think my body and mind found the resolve to succeed that day, as somewhere deep down some part of me realised this opportunity was a door cautiously opening. An escape. An out. Everything around and inside me was preparing to live and breathe again. Preparing the path to walk away. The universe, I believe, was working to manifest my heart's truest desire, the hunger for freedom and to be safe.

A few days after the screen test, the call of a job offer came through. When I told him e.tv was keen to have me join them, he told me in no uncertain terms he would break up with me if I took the job.

'That will be the end of us,' he said, 'so think carefully if that's what you want. You are for my eyes only, and now so many men will be looking at your face. Is that what you want – to have men look at you and lust over you?'

He had already made it clear that he despised my voice being heard on radio, so I should have known he would have been outraged by the thought of my face on television. Plus, he said, it would cheapen our relationship.

I quickly turned the job down. I told Dave Coles, the Durban bureau chief, I wasn't really interested in TV, plus the money on offer wasn't all that great, so I would happily stick to my current job. These were two good enough reasons and certainly better than the truth, which was that I was genuinely scared of taking it because of him. Scared not because he would break up with me, but scared because he would *stay* with me and make my life hell for taking the job. And no job, not even the prospect of being on television, was worth that.

That was until Debora Patta called me. She was the editor in chief at e.tv news at the time and a brand in her own right: a powerful journalist and woman, both admired and despised, depending which circles you moved in.

I was in awe. For a young woman journalist, she was a role model.

I would watch her on TV and wonder what it must feel like to be her. I would clap or laugh with absolute glee when she would extirpate those guilty of corruption. Her storytelling and journalism, as she exposed the ills of society, the suffering and the pain of those whose voices we choose not to hear, were burnt into my mind.

Debora was everything I wished I could one day be and never thought I would or could. And there she was, on the other end of the phone, talking to me.

And she expressed so much hope in me. I'd forgotten what it felt like to be flattered. To feel wanted. To feel needed. To feel important enough for someone like Debora to call me and talk me into joining the e.tv prime-time newsroom. I think there were moments during that call when my heart was thumping so loudly in my ears that I couldn't even hear a word of what she was saying.

Many years have passed, and that phone call from Debora has stayed with me. It was another marker on the path away from him and back to myself. Debora didn't know it at the time – and neither did I – but her phone call to me that day saved my life.

Debora had me sold, my two reasons for initially turning down the job quickly swiped away by her smooth talking. Money isn't an issue, she said. Give it six months, and we'll review it, she promised. And as for not wanting to be on TV, it's a new challenge, she said, this company is going places, and you'll do well to be part of it, as will we to have you on our team.

There was no arguing against that. There was no denying Debora Patta. Throughout my time at e.tv, while she was at the helm of the newsroom, I'd remain both in absolute awe and in constant fear of disappointing her. She didn't accept anything less than the best. The praises, when they came, didn't just lift me up, they catapulted me so high up, coming back down was hard. And the criticism didn't just cripple, it devastated. She was generous to a fault with both. But I was always eager to please. Experience had taught me that if I could make someone happy, then they'd have no reason to hurt me, with either their words or their fists. I was always trying to earn Debora's praises. I wasn't always successful, but hindsight has taught me that even in her moments of brutal honesty, she was always just pushing me to push myself even further to be the best version of myself as both a journalist and woman. In the end it wasn't her praises that moulded me into an award-winning journalist but her criticism that drove me to discover the beautiful things I was capable of producing when I pushed the boundaries of writing and presenting on television. When I pushed the boundaries of what I thought I was capable of.

It was Debora who picked up the phone that day in 2005 and called me. She threw me the lifeline. She bothered. Her belief in me gave me the ultimate confidence to do what I needed to do to save myself and live again.

I took the job only because the most powerful woman journalist in the country at the time believed in me and wanted me on her team. TV wasn't on the list of things I wanted to accomplish. But someone – and not just anyone – wanted me.

It was the start of a seven-year career that both mended and unravelled my soul. With television came fame, self-confidence and a sense of power. It opened my eyes and mind to the possibilities of a life without him.

But getting away wasn't going to be that easy. He never left me, like he had promised to, if I took the job. It would take that one last violent showdown in the SABC parking lot and a childishly simple plan from me to eventually walk away from him.

He needed me. He needed to run me down to elevate himself. I was his fix to feeling superior and indestructible. I was the fuel to his fire. So, he stuck around. It would take only a month, though before a battered face and a little resolve would sever all ties between us.

I started at e.tv in May 2005, an uneasy peace brokered between us. I was now out of his sight for most of the day. I was interacting with mostly men at my new workplace. I was careful not to give him any reason to hurt me. I didn't talk more than necessary to my new colleagues. Even though I knew there was no way he would find out if I were being friendly to the camera guys, I was still afraid. When you've been hit, slapped and punched just for smiling at another man, the fear of being friendly or doing anything that could trigger violence, even in the absence of your tormentor, never abates.

It's probably the worst kind of fear. It shrouds you. It follows you. It's in your head, your blood, flowing through you, a constant reminder that even when your abuser is out of sight, you're still shackled to him and his threats. You're still bound by his power and under his control, so you behave in a way not to endanger yourself, even when there is no way he'd ever know.

That's the ultimate control he wielded over me. Even when he wasn't around, I was programmed to keep the peace, not to do anything that could compromise myself or jeopardise my safety, so when he asked, 'Who did you speak to today?', I was able to answer truthfully. I know my eyes couldn't betray me, nor would there even be a slight rise in pitch in my voice to reveal me as a liar.

After the parking lot incident, I avoided him. But he was persistent. He would keep SMSing. One day he sent this message: 'Okay, you have had enough time. Don't overdo it.'

I couldn't blame him for thinking this was just another episode between us. This was always our routine dance of madness. He would hit me. I would break up with him, telling him I never wanted to see him again. He would apologise, imploring me to take him back, vowing to change and do better, convincing me with his 'I love yous', and I would relinquish all resolve to banish him from my life and allow him to con his way back in – only to do it all over again.

Over and over again this pathetic little exchange would play itself out, a bad movie on repeat. Beat me up, break up, reconcile. It is the dance of the abuser and the abused. As a victim I kept going back because my bruised and battered mind was trained to be dependent on the very person who inflicted the greatest trauma on me.

I imagine he thought this was simply a repeat performance of that boring act of trying to break free, but this time was different. As we weren't colleagues anymore, he was no longer in my space all day. Plus I had felt what it's like to have people see my worth and value as both a woman and a broadcaster. I had caught a glimpse of life without him, and I wanted more.

But shaking him off wasn't going to be easy. A few text messages would not be enough to sever all ties between us. I agreed to meet, so we could talk. He said he would pick me up from home. It was risky, as I knew how volatile he was and how unsafe it would be for me, but I took a chance.

I had a plan. It would take every ounce of sincerity and strength, neither of which I possessed at the time.

We drove into town, chatting about inane things, me deliberately skirting the most important reason for going out with him that evening. I sat in the passenger seat, where so many times before I had been slapped or shouted at. So many times before I'd cried and cringed in that seat. So many times before I sat in that seat, fearing for my life, clutching onto the sides, pressing my back and body into its curve, as he would pick up speed and drive recklessly in retaliation for something I'd said or for back chatting. So many times when he couldn't hit me, as he had to keep his hands on the wheel, he'd instil the fear of God into me by driving like a madman.

Recalling every single incident, I sat there that day, waiting, battling the panic and fear inside, weaving together what I wanted to say.

I had to have a talk with myself to speak the words I needed to say. I wasn't sure how he would take it. It could go one of two ways. He'd either accept, if I reasoned with him and presented my case like there was no other option, then back off for a while and finally convince me to take him back. Or he'd do what he had done several times before: hit me and tell me he'd never let me go and threaten to disrupt my life wherever I went, plus tell me that whomever I would go out with in future would live to regret ever setting eyes on me.

'We can't do this anymore,' I said, my voice soft and slow. 'Your mother has made it clear she will never accept me. I don't have it in me anymore to fight your parents. We can't go on like this hoping for them to come around to accepting us. It's never going to happen. You and I are never going to happen. And I am tired now. I love you, but I cannot do this anymore.'

I felt like I deserved an Oscar for that little performance. It sounded like I meant every single word.

I had met his mother a couple of months before. Both his parents disapproved of our relationship because I was raised in a different faith. But with his mother especially, that disapproval seemed to go beyond just religion to something more twisted and warped. I felt that she really despised me, and her contempt for me ultimately proved to be very useful. She gave me the perfect excuse to leave her son.

He kept saying we could make it, that his parents would eventually have no choice but to accept us. He even came up with a plan; he would marry the girl they chose for him, divorce her after a few months and tell them he couldn't be with her because he wasn't in love with her, and he would then come back to me – and they would have to accept it. Or he mused he could take me as a second wife. The first one would be for the benefit of his family, to keep his parents happy. I would be the real, loved wife, but I would have to be kept a secret. His faith made provisions for a man to take on a second or even third wife.

I was an educated, modern woman – and here he was suggesting I be part of some archaic practice.

'No,' I said, 'that is not going to work for me. I can't sit around waiting, for your parents to come around, for you to get married first. I don't want to be anyone's second wife.' I said softly, 'If we are meant to be we will find our way back to each other. But I don't believe it's God's plan for us to be together.'

If nothing else would convince him, the mention of God surely would, I thought. He took his belief in God very seriously, although even with God he would cheat. His double standards should have raised the red flag, but throughout our relationship, I chose not to see the warning signs.

He dropped me at home, probably still believing that after a few weeks apart we would get back together and not believing that I meant any of what I'd said.

I never set foot in his car again. We were done.

All things considered, it was a relatively clean break-up. Despite all the threats of never letting me go, of ruining my life if I ever left, he eventually let me walk away. For so many years I was trapped, stuck with him because of fear, because of the threats.

In the end I discovered they were nothing more than words spewed out to keep me chained. Those words only held as much power and meaning as I allowed them to. And it was *I* who gave those words power and meaning. With my actions and my feelings, I allowed those words and threats to have meaning. By being afraid, by believing his threats and his words, I empowered him and gave life to the things he said. I had created the monster. And I fed it with my fear.

I now just had to have the willpower to stay away for good this time. There were times I nearly gave in, where I wondered if I'd done the right thing. There were many times that I'd get SMSes lamenting our lost love, telling me how much he needed and missed me, and how miserable he was without me. If being with my abuser was painful, being away from him was excruciating. Especially when I got these messages. There were times when loneliness got the better of me, and I would have my phone in my hand typing out a message, a reply, saying I wanted to meet. But I quickly deleted them.

Like giving up any bad habit, you take it one day at time. I tried to quit smoking, on several occasions. The first day I would be all gung ho. By the second day I would become despondent, reasoning with myself that one cigarette wouldn't make a difference, it's just one. And an internal battle would rage between staying away and just having one. 'No one would know,' you tell yourself. 'What would be the big deal? You're in control and can stop anytime you want.' But if you want to kick a bad habit, you've got to make the decision to do it – and stick with it. Every second that passes becomes a victory, until those seconds become hours and days and weeks and months and years. But you have to take it one day at a time. And that's what I did with him.

I might have finally taken my leave from him, but I spent the next seven years on television making sure he would never forget my face or my name. I knew that as a regular on TV, I would be a constant presence and, more importantly, a reminder to him of how he ensnared me in his web of deceit and tainted love – and that he never really owned me at all.

Even if he switched off his television, he would not be able to escape me, as I often appeared in local print publications. There were very few Indian women on South African TV at the time, so newspapers and magazines were often vying to do features on this young Indian television-news reporter who was never without her trademark *bindi* (dot) or third eye. Everyone thought it was pretty. Hindu people admired this proud display of my religion. Worn between the eyebrows, the beautiful little adornment is meant to protect you from evil and bad luck. My *bindi* came to signify this and so much more for me. Putting it on every day, appearing on camera with it was my act of defiance and declaration of my emancipation. It was my quiet little message to just him: 'I have found my way back.' The *bindi* came to define me, and the media were telling the country everything about me, from how I was spending my Valentine's Day to what my New Year's resolutions were.

I did anything but slip into obscurity, which was what some of his friends no doubt expected to happen after we broke up. I'm convinced some of them, our colleagues at SABC, knew what was going on but kept their silence and their friendship with him, choosing to turn a blind eye to my bruises and scars.

Even now you can tune into a national radio station and hear them or watch them on television spewing their sanctimonious bull about women's rights and abuse from behind the pulpits of their microphones and all over their Twitter and Facebook feeds. But their inaction, their silence, their friendship with an abuser then – and even maybe now – makes them like so many others who choose not to get involved, equally culpable and complicit of the rot that prevails in our communities and homes. They worshipped him like a hero, which made what he did to me okay. They thought that I was the girl who struck it lucky by having him as a boyfriend and that he eventually came to his senses and ditched me. But they had it all wrong.

They would not forget my name, my face and my resilience. No, I made sure none of them would ever forget me. I made sure he would never forget. Disappearing silently and quietly was never an option for me.

# TWO

# Collision Course

When I look back at my life, I realise how every move, breath, choice and decision that I'd ever made was slowly leading me along a treacherous path into his orbit.

In 1999, I was accepted into the SABC's journalism internship programme at the Johannesburg studios in Auckland Park. I had graduated from journalism school the year before. Many of my fellow classmates struggled for a break, but I got incredibly lucky.

The naïve 22-year-old that I was, I'd forgotten to change my old phone number on the CV I submitted, along with a five-hundred-word essay on the future of broadcasting in South Africa, to the SABC. They loved it. I had been shortlisted for an interview. They had emailed the details, saying they were struggling to get a hold of me on the phone number on my CV.

I only saw the email a day after the interviews were done. I called and begged for another chance. They took my details but couldn't promise anything, because they had already chosen their candidates for the internship programme.

I was crushed. I couldn't believe how close I had come to having a foot in the door in a very difficult and cutthroat industry, never mind at the biggest broadcaster in the country.

But luck was truly on my side. Luck. What a strange word, given what would come. This lucky break was putting me on a collision course that would later come to alter the very essence of my being, rip my soul to shreds and leave me eternally tormented.

The next day I got a call from Kieran Maree, the internship coordinator. It was short and to the point: 'How soon can you get up to Johannesburg?'

After that things moved fast, so fast, I didn't really have time to savour any of it. My parents drove me up to Johannesburg from Durban. I had a thousand rands from my father to start me off – it was more money than he could afford. But he had a plan for his daughters. He had a dream for us girls. And he would drive himself to the grave making it happen.

Six months into the programme, I was transferred back to Durban to work as a radio news reporter at the local SABC bureau. I had just started to enjoy the big bustling city of Johannesburg in all its cosmopolitan glory and my independence. Sometimes I try to imagine what if I had insisted on staying on in Johannesburg. Would things have turned out differently? Or would I have just been postponing the inevitable?

I had a job. I was young. So I packed up my few belongings and half-heartedly headed back home. I was blissfully edging closer and closer towards him.

I did well as a radio reporter and quickly proved myself as a talented storyteller. My parents were very proud of me.

The SABC owns Lotus FM, a radio station that predominantly serves the Indian community. After a few weeks in Durban, I was scheduled to help put together content for Newsbreak, the daily current affairs programme on Lotus FM. It was the final move that threw me into the hemisphere of the man who would become my lover and tormentor for the next five years and seven months.

The production studio looked directly into the live Lotus FM studio, where DJs would change shifts every three hours. There was this one DJ, who was hard to miss. He was, I thought at the time, devilishly handsome. Tall, fair skinned and a real snazzy dresser. He walked into the studio like he owned it, with a swagger and a smile. Women in the newsroom swooned at the sight of him. I know, I was there, standing around, catching up on gossip. He would walk past, and we would talk to each other, but our eyes would travel the length of his body, deep breaths would be taken, as he would leave a trail of expensive fragrance in his wake. Naughty smiles and knowing looks would pass between us. Yes, women loved him. On the outside, he was perfectly put together. He was a beautiful specimen of a man.

I'd look up from the production studio and see him in the live studio, gesturing and talking animatedly into the microphone. I couldn't hear what he was saying, as the connection to the live studio was turned off while we were working on Newsbreak, but he looked so cool and debonair. I would be lying if I said I wasn't impressed by the show he put on.

We would often catch each other's eye through the glass window separating the studios. I would feel the heat creep up my skin, partly because I was shy, and partly because I couldn't believe he was making eye contact with this young, dark-skinned girl.

One afternoon he came waltzing into the production studio, lighting up a cigarette. I remember looking at the burning cigarette in his beautiful, well-manicured, piano-playing fingers and thinking how sexy they were. As was his devil-may-care attitude to the SABC's ban on smoking in the studio.

He started chatting to Ashok Ramsarup, one of the senior producers. I sat at the computer, half listening to their conversation through the headphones I had on and well aware that he kept throwing glances my way.

My mouth dried up and my heart quickened when I realised he had just asked me a question: 'So, when are we going out?'

It was the first time he had ever spoken to me, and that was the line he casually threw my way. Loaded and enticing, it lay suspended in the space between us.

I replied, 'Perhaps when you ask me!' Not missing a beat and very smoothly he named a day and time.

'Sure, why not?'

And so simply and easily it was done. Our threads had become entwined in a matter of seconds. And they would eventually grow to become a tangled web of deceit and destruction.

You can look into a person's face, even maybe get a glimpse of their soul and not see the darkness that resides within them. Maybe some people are just clever at keeping it hidden. Maybe some of us are too stupid to see or choose not to see.

I could never have foreseen what was to come though. And I wonder if I did if it would have mattered much to me at the time.

I was excited. He was cute. He was a DJ. Everyone spoke about him like he was some deep mystery. He was famous.

I was 22 years old and I had never had a boyfriend. I didn't usually do this kind of thing. Sure, I would sit and ogle the cute guys with my girlfriends at Technikon, but that's about as exciting as life got. I had no interest in any of the boys who asked me out then. So yes, I didn't usually do this kind of thing.

I wanted to fall in love. I was filled with romantic and perhaps rather outdated notions of life and love.

But the first date wasn't earth shattering. We took his car after work and went out for supper. He ate, and I just had something to drink. I was attempting to be sophisticated, and scoffing down food in front of this guy I barely knew and opening myself to the possibilities of getting something stuck in my teeth was too frightening. I was in a busy restaurant, having my first real date with a guy. And not just any guy – one of the hottest guys at the SABC in Durban and certainly one of the hottest Lotus FM DJs.

I watched him tuck into his meal of prawns and rice, my stomach grumbling, protesting my feigned disdain to eat. I went home that night and stuffed my face. In fact, the entire date I couldn't wait to go home and eat.

He did most of the talking. I was content to watch and listen. Well, not really content to watch, because I was bloody famished.

Heading back to the office afterwards, he stopped in the middle of a road in a quiet suburb and asked me if he could kiss me. How utterly cheesy, I thought. I felt a little embarrassed for him and squirmed a little in my seat. Thank God, I hadn't eaten and had been chewing gum, so I wouldn't have to worry about my breath. The dilemmas of dating.

'Maybe,' I answered coquettishly.

Any expectation I had of butterflies and fireworks were pretty much crushed. He didn't set my skin on fire. No quickening of my pulse, racing of my heart or goose bumps – it was an uneventful kiss, bland and uninspiring. He was good looking, and that's where it ended. Good looking does not always equal sparks. So, I never thought there would be another date or kiss, or anything else, for that matter.

I was waiting, saving myself for the One Great Love. So, I struck him off my mental list as soon as we parted ways after that dismal date.

But he called later that night and said he wanted to go out again. And I said yes. It was like my mouth was working on its own accord with no connection to my brain at all.

The moment my mother found out I was going on a date with a guy of a different faith, she blew her top. I had to tell her, because he was going to come and pick me up from home for our second date. She warned me profusely against pursuing a relationship with someone from outside our religion.

This was only the second date, for God's sake, and my mother was acting like we were getting married. My mother – and most Indian mothers – believed that if you go out with someone, there must be a good chance that it will eventually lead to marriage. You don't just go out on multiple dates with a guy and not marry him! No, in the Indian community, we don't do dating. The Indian etiquette is for your parents to find you a suitable match, arrange a proposal that could translate into the suitable partner and his parents rocking up at your house, often under the guise of coming over for tea or a meal, but it's actually a formal meeting of the prospective partners. After the meeting the two mothers call each other for feedback, and should both boy and girl like what they see, well then, the deal is sealed. There could perhaps be a courting of some sort and a discussion around marriage dates. Parents consider a whole host of things when they consider matches for their kids; religion, of course, is top of the list.

So for my traditional, conservative mother who was very mindful of how outsiders would view our internal family matters, the idea of her daughter going on dates with a man of a different religion was hard to accept. But I was the youngest, and she made some allowances for me – and for the changing times. Grudgingly, she gave in.

But, in typical Indian-mother style, she went on to blackmail me emotionally. After a few more dates, she threatened not to come to my wedding if I ever married him. It hadn't even been a month that he and I had been going out, we barely knew each other's favourite colour – and here she was already talking about a wedding. Thank goodness that never happened.

But we took things further, of course. That December, he regularly waited for me until my shift ended. We went out, or he drove me home sometimes. It was the month that I took my rather archaic beliefs about love and life, folded them up and stowed them away at the back of my head. It was time to move on, live a little and grow up. No waiting for love or marriage.

That poignant moment in a young girl's life as she stumbles into becoming a woman in a matter of seconds, that precious fleeting moment when innocence reluctantly and painfully makes way for that taboo and wondrous thing called sex, turned out to be embarrassingly clichéd for me. I would later realise just how painfully naïve I had been, how utterly stupid and gullible.

I should have waited. I should have never compromised on my standards and the things I believed in. I always wanted my first time to be with someone special, with the person with whom I would spend the rest of my life. It was the rule I lived by. I was influenced in large parts by the stern warnings issued by my mother to remain chaste and wait for marriage. Sex before marriage is generally vilified in traditional Indian communities, and as a young girl you're told never to even contemplate the dastardly act until you're lying on your marital bed ready to consummate the vows taken earlier that day.

'Don't spoil yourself. Don't embarrass the family,' I was told, all these cautions uttered to protect the sanctity of my virginity. Growing up with these rigid rules, and probably reading too many romance novels, I was fairly prudish. While lots of girls I knew were already sexually active in high school, some as young as 14 (because despite the rigid rules of our conservative little community, we are, once all the veneer of propriety is stripped away, just normal human beings with faults and fantasies but that is a thing best kept secret), I had yet to even kiss a boy.

I wanted it all. I wanted to love and be loved. I wanted fireworks and butterflies. I was out of touch with reality and with life. That summer of 1999, I became the ultimate cliché, in the backseat of a car with a guy who told me it was also his first time. I believed him. And I allowed myself to be led to a place where the one thing I valued and prided myself on – that defined me and set me apart from my friends and many young girls around me, that I held onto – was taken away in minutes in the backseat of a car with the sound of the sea and the humidity of a sultry Durban night filling my ears and my senses.

It was uncomfortable, awkward, painful, and I cried. Because this was not how I envisioned my first time. I wept for all that I was losing. I mourned the moment that I could never undo before it was even done.

Later, after spending much time in his company and coming to know his arrogance, I realised he probably would have thought they were tears of joy and pleasure. But there was nothing pleasurable or even profound about that grand moment. In fact, it was an absolute anti-climax.

For someone who claimed it was also his first time, he sure knew what he was doing. No fumbling and stumbling. He was casual and blasé. He never even stopped to ask if I was okay or in pain, even as I squirmed and whimpered. In a few minutes he was done. He later flippantly asked me if I was sure it was my first time, because I seemed to know what I was doing.

The way he did things that night became common practice in the years we were together. It was the only way I would understand and experience the ultimate physical connection with another human being.

His sexual gratification was all there was between us. No matter how I would feel, no matter the tension between us, no matter the tears trailing down my face, no matter the hatred that would course through my veins and fill my head, if and when he was in the mood, I would have to relinquish whatever it was I would be feeling and surrender to the deftness of his hands and the roughness of him claiming and taming my body.

I remember occasions when my head was forced down to his lap, as he sat in the driver's seat of his car. I was pushed to my knees, which always seemed unbendable. My unyielding mouth was doing things to give him pleasure, and I was pretending, always pretending. I was a wretched young girl on her knees, on her back. Porn gave him ideas to up the ante of his sexual thrill. I objected, sometimes aloud, sometimes silently, but I always submitted in the end. While I was with him, I never quite understood that sex, the moulding of two bodies, should be a mix and manifestation of physical pleasure and spiritual enlightenment. Sex should be a profound solace found in the arms, the touch and the gaze of someone who shows their love by worshipping your body, not defiling it with their debauchery. His brand of love commanded and demanded me to do things I never quite enjoyed or wanted to do.

So many times I would lie beneath him, my mind travelling to places far beyond where I was in that moment. I would shut my eyes and clench my jaws, imagining someone else, pretending it was someone else. I could escape from the physical place my body was in by allowing my mind to drift far away. It was how I clutched onto my sanity, learnt to lie to myself that the whole act was pleasurable, deceive myself that it was all okay and that I was a willing participant – especially in those moments when I didn't want to be intimate with him and had no choice, but saying no was just not possible.

When the deed was done the first time around, it sealed my loyalty and ties to this man without my even knowing it or making a conscious decision about it. By then, he and I were in a relationship. I was his girlfriend, and he was my boyfriend. I believed the title of girlfriend prohibited any objections to any acts however deplorable or detested. My first lover instilled in me the idea that both love and sex were things meant to be taken – even by force – and for his pleasure alone. I was bound to him, because he owned the one thing that was my pride and my honour. I was a street-smart girl, but I was desperately antiquated in my beliefs about chastity and love.

I chose poorly and badly. But I had chosen nonetheless and accepted to share something so intense with someone who deemed the backseat of his car the best, most romantic and poignant spot to do so.

It could never be undone, that definitive moment when a young girl becomes a woman.

And when I later found out that I was not his first, as he had claimed, it drove the knife of betrayal even deeper. It made me feel completely worthless and stupid, and grieving the loss of my virginity to someone so vile and contemptuous.

I was also slowly being exposed to his fame. He loved talking about it, recounting how listeners would call in and tell him how much they loved his show and only listened to Lotus FM because of him. He boasted about mothers telling him they wished their sons could be like him and women propositioning him. He bragged to me that listeners offered him sex. The women who did this though did seem to have some sense of etiquette, making their indecent proposals off air and never on live radio. Otherwise, all the old aunties listening in would probably keel over and die!

At first I felt like, 'Wow, this famous guy is with me.' I was thrilled for him and basked in his glory and success. But soon it became downright irritating and annoying. I remember watching him preening himself in front of the mirror, practising his dance moves and facial expressions before one of the Lotus FM bhangra bashes (Indian dance parties) and thinking how ridiculous it all was. He seemed to fashion himself around one of his favourite Bollywood actors, Shah Rukh Khan. I had never even heard of Shah Rukh, let alone watched a Bollywood movie till I started dating him. He looked at himself in the mirror and threw simpering looks of exaggerated adoration just like the Bollywood stars do during those very chaste love scenes. All that was missing in that moment was a tree for him to run around. I thought it was hilarious, but I knew a girlfriend should not laugh at her boyfriend, so I would stifle my giggles and try to mask my disbelief and smile with what I hoped was a look of admiration.

His fame also began to diminish me, making me feel insecure and unsure, especially his bragging about listeners wanting to sleep with him. I sometimes felt he would at any moment take someone up on her offer.

So, with this constant barrage of boasting and my insecurity, it wasn't too long before we had our first argument. It was in January 2000, that much I can remember. We had been dating for just over a month. But even if I tried, I can't recall what the fight was about. I'm sure it was related to girls and his interaction with women calling in. After the fight, I avoided his calls and SMSes for a while.

As I was leaving the building after my shift one evening, he showed up, grabbed my bag and walked out of the building. I followed, and he ordered me into his car. I never felt any sense of danger. I never thought I couldn't trust him. I was just angry that he had taken my bag and I was being forced to now talk to him when I was still stewing over our fight.

Once we were inside the car, the air shifted, a subtle change that I was oblivious to because I didn't know what was coming. He was busy driving out of the parking lot. I think I was talking, a little too loudly and passionately perhaps.

Suddenly, out of nowhere, his fist slammed into my chest. My talking ceased. Silence. At first, I wasn't even sure what had just happened. Or perhaps I didn't want to believe what had just happened. I was in such shock, the physical pain and the fact that he was shouting at me didn't register. I'm not sure if he'd been shouting at me all the while. I'm not sure of anything except the moment his fist slammed into my chest. That dashing, debonair DJ, that popular if somewhat pompous radio presenter, was shouting like a madman. Surely this wasn't happening? Surely this didn't just happen?

I sat there, numb and in silence, heat creeping up my face, a thousand thoughts somersaulting inside my head – I had just been punched in the chest. By my boyfriend. It was the first time he hit me, and it would of course not be the last, but I didn't know that at the time.

When the reality sunk in, I managed a sob, more out of disbelief and shock than actual pain.

The sound immediately stopped his ranting. The mood shifted again. The air became less tense. We had reached a spot where he could park.

And the apologies came pouring out of his mouth quick and fast; he even cried. He sobbed. He was so sorry; he had never done anything like that before, he said. I shifted and agonised in my seat, unsure, even a little embarrassed that I had caused this to happen. We were, for all intents and purposes, still relative strangers. Our relationship was still in its infancy.

Eyes brimming with tears, he looked at me and asked if I was going to leave him. He said he would deserve it if I did. His demeanour was dejected, it really was: shoulders slumped, head bowed down, crestfallen. Everything to suggest he himself couldn't believe what had just happened. That he was horrified and deeply distressed by what he had just done.

But as I searched his eyes and face, they were devoid of anything sincere. He was talking, he was crying, he was saying all the right things, his throaty voice oozed with regret, but somehow it all just looked and sounded contrived. I should have run. I should have run and never looked back.

I knew what he did was wrong, that he wasn't for me, that I didn't even like him, that I didn't buy his apology. But even as the shock of that first punch still reverberated through my chest, even as the realisation of that act of violence tried to settle inside my brain, he uttered three words that snaked their way into my head and heart and wound themselves tightly around me, leaving me breathless and blinding me to the enormity of what had just happened.

'I love you,' he said. His words sent a rush through me, calmed me and stilled my racing thoughts. They sent waves of heat cascading through my body. These were powerful words that ignited every nerve in my body. He felt so intensely for me, he explained, that it drove him insane when I didn't answer his calls or text messages.

And even though it sounded like a well-rehearsed line, I still fell for it. I fell without even a second thought about what he'd just done to me. I fell willingly, I fell deep and hard and without feeling an ounce of the love *he* claimed to feel.

I was reeling from hearing those words. I had been waiting and hoping for love. I wanted the stuff of romance novels that I would read in the quiet of my bedroom as a teenager. Damn those Mills & Boon novels! I wanted someone to make me feel beautiful.

It's what I had been chasing for such a long time, to be beautiful enough for someone to love and want. And there it was, a guy so many other girls were pining after offering it to me.

On the outside he was everything. On the outside he was written for the part to be my forever guy. He was perfect on paper. But paper can cut.

And against my better judgement, I reached over and gathered him in my arms and held him. He buried his face into my neck and held me back. Tightly. I said I was sorry and, no, I would never leave him. How could I? How could I leave him? He was my first lover. He would be my only. I would learn to love him the way he just said he loved me.

Governed by that ridiculous unspoken rules of my community, I slept with him, so I was stuck with him.

But as I held him and felt his heat seep into my clothes and onto my skin, I felt nothing. I felt empty, like I was playing a part in a badly scripted play. I held him tight and told him it was all okay. I was convinced I drove him to this, so I was obliged to be the peacemaker. And I really thought it was okay; the punch wasn't that hard.

He just told me what I'd been waiting to hear, that he loved me. I didn't necessarily want to hear those words from him, but he had been the one to deliver them to me, gentle words that flowed from his mouth, that sought to erase the violence of the unexpected fist that had landed on my chest a few minutes before. The punch? Well, he did say sorry, and I had been quite obstinate, I thought.

This was love. This was how it was supposed to be, I told myself. You don't just break up for a small little fight. This must be what it's like for all couples. When there's arguing and fighting, someone is bound to get a little emotional. That's what happens when you feel strongly about someone. Plus, I really should never have ignored him.

His tears left a wet patch on my shirt – proof of his regret.

Then the thoughts started coming thick and fast: How could I not feel bad? After all, this was my fault. I should never have ignored him. There was no one to blame but myself. And really it was all okay. He didn't really hurt me, and I was sure he would never do it again. He loved me after all. He had just said so. And now that I knew that he loved me, and from all the girls he could be with, he chose me, I could start working at being more supportive and less insecure. I could commit all of me and not feel threatened because some silly listener is calling him and offering herself to him. He was just sharing all these stories with me because I was his girlfriend. Stupid me for thinking he was deliberately trying to hurt me and chisel away at my self-confidence by boasting about his popularity.

That night, by accepting his apology, offering one of my own and promising never to leave him, I committed myself to a dangerous man and a doomed relationship. Because that's whom he showed himself to be in the days, weeks, months and years to come, a dark force of energy that leeched off me in every possible way and drained me of all confidence. A man who would continuously mould, shape and bend me as he willed and wanted, and who could make me feel seen and loved in one moment, and in the next make me feel insignificant and afraid with his words and his fists.

But all of that, how loved and special and happy I could feel, how wasted and worthless I would feel, were my own thoughts and emotions, even though they were triggered by his actions. It was a huge burden to bear, a responsibility that I never quite mastered.

# THREE

# *Breaking the Silence*

Post-traumatic stress is a very real thing. Sometimes we don't know it by its name, but even nameless things can be debilitating and destructive. More than a decade after our relationship ended, I still wake up with images of a violent encounter lingering in my head. I can still wake up and cry remembering just one incident.

I sometimes dream of being back at the SABC, and after I rise from my fitful sleep, the terror of being back, working in the same building and being near him follows me into my waking world. Sometimes I wake up unsure of what happened the night before, not understanding why I feel so distraught and in such a rage. I try and recall if I had a fight with someone.

These feelings can sometimes come from nowhere, when I least expect them. It is like being kicked and punched all over again. It never abates. You just learn to manage and smile through it. You learn to live with it – either that or you simply surrender and break into a million pieces over and over again.

But in remembering and writing, I am finally acknowledging what was done to me and what I allowed to happen to me. In doing this I mend myself.

I can't reach peace if I don't break my silence. I have never had therapy for the abuse, and I have never spoken in such painful and explicit detail about it as I am doing here. I don't want to keep this secret anymore. I don't want to keep his secret anymore. Or maybe it has only been my secret all this while. It has weighed me down. And every second of every day that I have kept this inside me, it has made me complicit in the lies and the abuse. I can't do it anymore.

You can never be free while you cling to the past. You may think you have moved on and achieved degrees of success. You may have found love. You may smile and laugh. But you're never totally free. Not until you release the memories and voice the suffering, the trauma. Not until you've acknowledged your fears and anguish, you remain imprisoned. No amount of fame or fortune can bail you out.

No, freedom comes at a price. To be really and truly free one has to confess to being a liar, admit to the lies and ultimately become subservient to the brutal truth. To be free you must turn your back on public perception and become the purveyor of that truth. Deliver it from the darkest places inside your soul and your head where it lives. Bring forth the truth, so that it can breathe without you having to mask it with lies every moment you live. To be emancipated, you must allow that truth to be told once and for all.

By telling my story, I understand that I am breaking the unspoken laws that govern many Indian families and most within my community. We're not supposed to talk about things like this. A revelation of this nature is deemed embarrassing. These sorts of things are best kept quiet and forgotten about. We self-censor because, God forbid, what would people say if they find out?

What will other people think? For many in the Indian community, the opinions of others are a mark of one's social standing. What others think often trumps your own sense of right and wrong – and even your right to happiness. I think I have a liberated lifestyle and views, yet I catch myself living my life not according to what rocks my boat but to how others would view it. We're a judgemental lot, really, myself included.

It's quite a pickle, being an Indian woman who's been abused, plus someone in the public eye. To an extent, I stress about what the next person is going to say and think, but I am ultimately driven by a force greater than all of that – the need to come clean, speak my truth and own my story. The need to speak out and break the silence, share and ease my own burden. And, above all, the need to set a new precedent and change the rules of being an Indian woman and being a victim.

Silence disempowers the victim and empowers and enables the perpetrator. Silence diminishes the victim and emboldens the abuser. Silence says it's okay. Silence protects the people who least deserve protection. But more than that, silence says you are afraid. You're afraid of the person who abused you and that no one will believe you. Silence speaks more than it says.

This is my story. This happened to me. Who he is, is irrelevant. He could be the boy next door, a street sweeper or your son – he could be anyone. I refuse to make this story about him or who he is. He is no different to any other abusive man. His name is irrelevant. What he did to me, though, is relevant. What he did to me – over and over again – is very relevant.

This is South Africa. It is 2018. My story is one of hundreds of thousands of women, many of whom are silent and don't have the courage to speak out, because they are simply too afraid. I know their fear. I've known it, lived with it all these years, following me, hanging over my shoulder, filling my head. Fear when I am in close confines with or in the middle of an argument or heated discussion with any man. Even with men who I know would rather die before ever raising a hand to me, I find myself inwardly recoiling.

My fear is entrenched. It used to ride in cars with me when I would go out on stories with cameramen. It would go on dates with me, hovering like an annoying chaperone. Fear has made a mate of me for life. I am tired of being afraid. I refuse to remain silent, a victim. I survived.

I live to tell the tale.

I am cutting through the stigma and battling the courts of public opinion. I'm ripping open my soul and baring it for all to see. I'm doing it for the women who couldn't and didn't. For the women who never made it out and whose lives were cut short and whose dreams will forever remain unfulfilled. For their families, whose lives have been forever altered because of a jealous and abusive lover. For the countless other women before me, and those who will come after me. Because there will always be others.

As an Indian woman, I'm doing the unthinkable and possibly the unforgiveable. But in a country grappling with astoundingly high levels of violence against women and children, I will make no apologies. I owe my honesty, however embarrassing some may deem it to be, to all the women of every race group who never made it out alive. I was lucky. I must speak my truth even in the face of disbelief. I must own my truth, because truth is all we have. It's what defines us. It's the one thing that no one can take away: the truth, your truth, my truth. Not denials, not disbelief. Nothing can diminish the truth.

For every day that I live and laugh and love, I owe a debt to my community and my country to speak out. I owe a debt to every woman who has ever been slapped, punched, kicked and – worse – killed by her partner. And I always settle my debts.

I could have ended up dead. And I cannot squander the second chance I'd been given. I will not waste it.

Why has it taken me so long to do this? For starters, I found it hard to accept that I allowed this to happen to me. In fact, I still do. I believed in forgetting about it and moving on. But how can you truly ever move on when your truth is trapped? How can you ever be truly free when you remain bound and shackled to your past? When it has followed you through the days and years, when it hounds you in both your waking and dream worlds. I let my past go, but it has never let me go. It is that little bit of poison that lingers in your system, sullying the good and the happy times.

My story has also taken some time to be told, because I was afraid. Of him, of the truth, of what people would say. But of what value is a life lived in fear? And how best to vanquish fear but to face it and call it by its name. I think of him as a sad human being who seemed to only feel empowered by demeaning me. Such a man should not be feared. When your strength and superiority as a man is derived from the weeping of a bleeding, battered and broken woman, then do you not deserve to be pitied? Because here's the thing, you would have to be broken and damaged to inflict that kind of trauma and pain on another human being.

I have been emboldened by women around the world coming out with their truth of physical, verbal and sexual abuse. From Hollywood to the informal settlements in South Africa, survivors are coming out, their abusers ranging from respected and revered movie bosses to presidents. These women have been my motivation. The time for keeping secrets is clearly over. The time for the truth is here.

I started writing before the #MeToo Movement gained momentum, sweeping around the globe and making it easier to talk publicly about one's personal pain and trauma. I wrote to release, unsure if I wanted anyone knowing the full extent of my private shame. And then #MeToo made me realise the power I held in my hands and my words. Those famous women who spoke out empowered me, so I see it as my duty to speak out and empower others.

Did it hurt to remember and write about it? I felt nothing. There was no sorrow, no grief and no pain. I remembered it all too vividly, but I struggled still, to feel any connection to that young girl who got kicked, punched and slapped. Yes, I pitied her and the fact that it was me who allowed her to endure that humiliation for so many years. It was hard for me to mourn or grieve for her.

But I did find myself weeping uncontrollably as I typed my recollections and I wondered why that was. It couldn't be because that gaping wound was still festering and bleeding in moments of solitude. I think I cried because I never really got to cry back then. All the pent-up tears just caught up with me, I think. That was all that it was. That is how I pacified myself. I was not crying for myself or for that girl.

It sometimes felt like I had dreamt it all. Maybe I had. Maybe this was all some horrible nightmare that had gone on for too long, a nightmare in which I had become stuck. Maybe I dreamt him up. Maybe he never really existed. Maybe I was just a sad, lonely, pathetic girl desperate for love and wrote this twisted warped story about this misunderstood man inside my head. It certainly felt like it. It has always felt like it. This struggle of mine to connect with that abused girl.

Even when I remained trapped in the throes of passion and abuse, there was never any connection between my physical and emotional self. I was two separate girls inhabiting one abused body.

I fear I still fail that abused girl. But I'll tell you her story with unreserved, brutal honesty. It's perhaps all I can do to make peace with her and let her know that I truly am sorry. Because I am.

I feel my unborn child stir beneath my skin as I type feverishly, almost as if my dark thoughts and memories of violence are entering that safe space the baby keeps in my womb. This is my third child. It is 2017.

I started writing this book in 2015. I was pregnant with my second child. The weight of the trapped words and memories of what had happened had finally made a crack in me and had come spilling out: messy, ugly, bitter. So much so that it travelled from the space inside my head to every part of me, tainting me and the world I lived in and making me feel angry and spent. I could even taste its foulness on my tongue, sour and sharp. It was the taste of regret, of sorrow.

It was taking me to a dark place, one that I wasn't afraid of, but writing this and remembering every incident physically affected me. Nightmares of being back at the SABC and running into him in the lift or the car park flooded my slumber, and continued into my waking world. My heart pounded in my chest, my body raged with fever. Who knew dreams could have such a profound physical effect on a person? I became moody, morose and angry for no reason. I could only put it down to me going back in my head to my days at Lotus FM with him. I had to stop writing.

It took me more than two years to open the initial draft again and continue. This time, I do it not out of anger but determination and resolve.

What has happened has happened. There is no undoing it. I could never undo it. But I can make amends, and while I'm not so sure about this clichéd 'everything happens for a reason' comment that people make when they hear about something bad, I believe I can't have endured what I did for nothing.

I want to be a voice and a beacon of hope.

I built a safe room for the abuse. I guarded it fiercely all these years. I'm taking down those walls and liberating myself.

This is as much a story for my children as it is for my mother and sisters who stood steadfast beside me and my husband – the man who would slowly and painstakingly mend my broken bits with unreserved patience and devotion many years after the abuse.

This story is penance for my past. And maybe, just maybe, it will reach deep into your core and give you a glimmer of hope. If you're now where I used to be, then this is your story too.

I don't need pity because I survived. I walked away. A few tiny scars, almost invisible and fading. Sometimes ghost pains and aches in places where I recall a fist slamming into my face or forehead, the mind perhaps playing tricks on the physical self, a polite reminder, if you will, of what I allowed to happen to me.

I'll show you it's possible to live, laugh and love. It comes gently, it comes unannounced like most good things, but it does come.

Helpless and hopeless? I was led to believe I was.

Getting slapped around and being constantly berated became the norm in our relationship. But don't get me wrong. As much as there was so much misery, he and I also enjoyed some happy highs.

When things were good, they were great. We got on like a house on fire. We laughed insanely, danced and drank. Yes, he was devout, and his religion forbids alcohol, but I thought perhaps his god makes exceptions, just as his staunchest followers sometimes do.

He would pull up to the bottle store and send me in, as he couldn't be seen anywhere near a liquor store. I could also get into trouble if a relative or family friend saw me. Within the generally conservative Indian community some things are best kept hidden. Girls drinking would fall into that category. You certainly don't go around advertising that you enjoy drinking, and walking into a liquor store would be just that. No, you keep these kinds of things hidden and enjoy the pleasures of taboo things while portraying the veneer of absolute respectability. It's really a case of what they don't know can't hurt them.

When I was reluctant to go into the bottle store, he said it wouldn't be so bad for me because I was Tamil. Since he was so recognisable, it would be professional and personal suicide for him to be caught in a bottle store. So I would relent.

As liberated as we both thought we were in our thinking and behaviour, we were still like two school kids up to no good and always going to great lengths to keep it hidden. After all, what would the people say?

I enjoyed those fleeting moments of happiness. That's what kept me holding on, as those moments instilled in me the belief that I could change him, that I could inspire him to be a better and gentler man.

Every time he hit me, I believed it would be the last. I sincerely believed in his potential and his promise to do and be better and treat me right. I had to believe in that for the sake of my own sanity. To believe otherwise would be admitting how utterly wrong I'd been and accepting that I was one of *those* women.

I believed I could subdue the raging beast. But there was always a dark cloud that hovered above us. And I was constantly clutching onto the fragile peace between us, willing it to last and trying my best never to upset it. But in an abusive relationship, the good times, the heartfelt apologies, the expensive gifts, the flowers and certainly not the promises of never doing it again don't count for much. Flowers die, perfumes dry up and lose their scent, and words… Well, words are really just words. Nothing but syllables and letters strung together.

All these things are superficial salves that soothe the scars and the hurt and attempt to make amends for a moment of violence. The same words are spewed out over and over again until their meaning is beaten into submission, until they become empty sounds uttered to confuse. The gifts become treacherous trinkets that make you doubt yourself and walk back willingly into the arms of the person who beats you. Forgiveness comes cheap.

For those on the outside, who have never suffered abuse and never lived in fear, it's perhaps easy to judge. But it's hard to really know what it's like for us emotionally, physically and mentally. From the outside staying or leaving might appear to be a choice, but how much of a choice is it truly when you have subtly and cleverly been programmed to stay? Your choice has already been made for you and not by you. Choice is an illusion.

Leaving is never easy. Walking away is not always possible. Because your abuser doesn't just hurt you physically, your abuser strips you of all common sense, your ability to rationalise, to see right from wrong. Most of all, your abuser will have already extinguished all your confidence, and without confidence how can you possibly have the courage to do what you know you should do?

Fear is the main source of control. When you're afraid, it's your abuser that offers the greatest security. Without your abuser, you'll be alone. And you feel that if people found out your secret, no one will believe you, love you as much or want you. And so you stay, and you hope, and you pray. You stay, you hate, and you try not to cause another violent eruption. You stay because there's no alternative. Or so it seems.

And all along you change. I know I did. Despite my somewhat conservative upbringing, I wasn't your typical Indian girl. I was my own person. I used to be headstrong and opinionated, an extrovert. I had lots of friends. I laughed with wild abandon. I was daring with what I wore, much to my mother's dismay. She often made clothes for me, and despite her distaste for my skimpy designs and protestations over what I wore, she made them nonetheless, while muttering under her breath, grudgingly acknowledging that I actually looked cute. I had loads of attitude. I spoke my mind. I was unconventional and untamed. And people were drawn to that wildness. That was before the beatings began.

Those qualities seemed to rile him up. Baring my arms was disgraceful, wearing a short skirt was disgusting, and just talking to other men was a betrayal. All these things, he said, meant I had no morals, no values and certainly no respect for him. The walls were continuously closing in on me. Just when I would think I had it figured out and that I knew what not to do to avoid upsetting him, something new would come up. I could never seem to get a handle on things. I really tried to stop doing the things I knew would cause him to erupt, and I would be pleased with myself because I knew no short skirts would spell peace and not being friendly with my male work colleagues would make him happy. But just when I thought I'd got it right, I would do something to make him turn on me. I was always 'making him' turn on me.

Never mind that he drank, went clubbing and, as I would later learn, had sex with a string of partners, most of whom were not of the same faith as he was. He was self-righteous and indignant, constantly trying to instil acceptable behaviour in me.

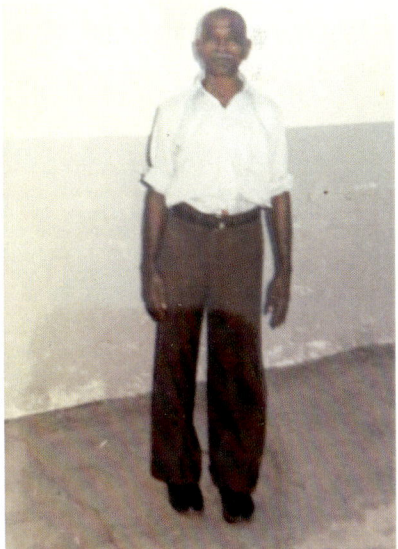

TOP: *Mom and Dad on their wedding day, 17 January 1965*

BOTTOM LEFT: *My paternal great grandfather, Thambooran Gounden, (middle) with my parents on their wedding day*

BOTTOM RIGHT: *My paternal grandfather Vurdan Govender, 1967*

TOP: *Dad and seven-month-old me*

BOTTOM: *My father (far left) as a waiter at the Blue Waters Hotel*

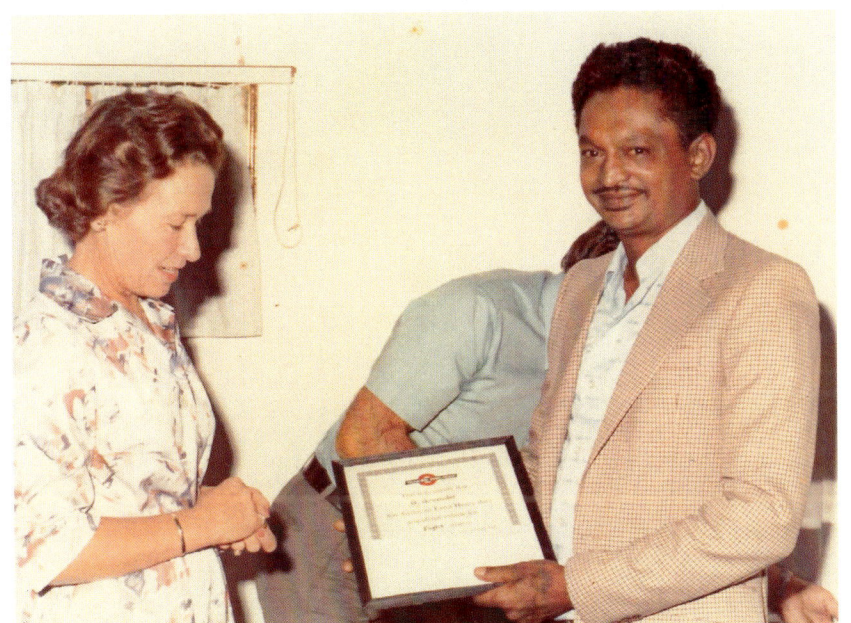

TOP: *My dad receiving an award for his outstanding driving record at Tanker Services*

MIDDLE: *My dad (third from left) as a bus driver*

LEFT: *My father with one of the large Tanker Service trucks that he drove*

TOP LEFT: *Birthday celebrations for Preshene and Rita, 1975*

TOP RIGHT: *My parents and one-year-old me outside No 807 Bellair Road in Cato Manor. Our tin house was located behind this main building, which housed all my father's siblings and their children.*

BOTTOM: *At age five, with Zebbie, our neighbour's dog, 1982*

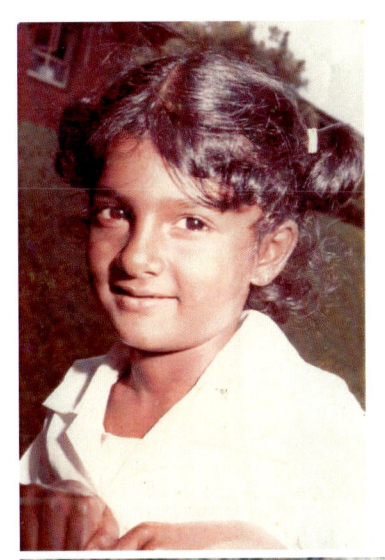

TOP: *Grade 1, Erica Primary School, 1983*
BOTTOM: *Fourteen years old, 1991*

TOP: *Rita and I, 1995*

BOTTOM: *With Mom and Dad, 1994*

TOP: *Graduation day, 1998*
BOTTOM: *Happy times with mom, 2010*

*With former Lotus FM Newsbreak senior producer Ashok Ramsarup in 2015*

He didn't have to say it, but his admonishment of me when I wore something he considered inappropriate, like a sleeveless top, or when I expressed my thoughts about something that had just happened in the news, seemed to indicate he felt women should not have opinions. If my opinion differed from his, he would get incensed, accusing me of deliberately wanting to contradict him. 'No,' I would say, flabbergasted and flummoxed, 'it's just how I view it or what I think. No hidden agendas,' I would try to pacify him. But in time I learnt to nod my head in agreement, never to say anything that could be misconstrued as being contradictory. My opinion was really not worth a slap. I could keep it to myself. It would be safer.

He wasn't always like that though. In the beginning, there was nothing to suggest he was anything but cool and open-minded, unhindered by the confines of his religion. But time has a way of compelling people to show their true colours. All the private dark quirks they keep hidden always have a way of surfacing.

Over time it started happening. If I didn't agree with what he said or do as he asked, or if I spoke to male colleagues or wore something remotely sexy or short, it would trigger an argument and often a slap or two. And the violence would be spaced out, so it took a while before I started to see a pattern, understood that something was wrong and see him for the controlling monster that he was.

One time he ripped a shirt right off my back as we sat inside his car in the SABC parking lot. It was made of a very flimsy, transparent fabric. You could see my camisole through it. It wasn't even my shirt; it was my sister Rita's, and I'd worn it that day without asking her. It's one of the perks of having sisters; we raided each other's wardrobes, often without asking. And as the youngest, I was often indulged when I dressed myself from Rita or Preshene's wardrobes without asking their permission first.

The moment he laid eyes on me that morning, he looked angry. I could read the displeasure in his eyes, the disapproval in his clenched jaws. But it was just a shirt. I really didn't think he'd be upset over a silly shirt. Anyway, there was nothing vulgar or overtly sexy about it. Well, not to me. But his anger festered as the day wore on.

And then it erupted. He asked me where I got it from, and couldn't I see how disgusting it looked? All the other DJs at Lotus FM would be laughing behind his back, he said, because his girlfriend was exposing herself to everyone. I laughed, more from disbelief than anything. I couldn't believe he'd just said that. It was ludicrous to say the least. No part of my body was exposed. Yes, it was transparent, but I was wearing a camisole underneath. My laugh was cut short as he savagely pulled at the shirt. It didn't take too much effort for it to tear, the loud rip triggering my anger.

Something in my brain was switched on, like a key being turned in the ignition of a car. And I went berserk. I started lashing out. This wasn't even my shirt, and this miserable fucker had torn it. I thought I would just wear it and wash it, quietly put it back into my sister's cupboard and she would be none the wiser. I was furious, and I fought back. The two of us locked in battle within the confines of a tiny sports car. I was all hands and feet as I blindly hit and kicked at whatever part of him I could reach. He continued ripping the shirt, his fingers scratching me, and his hands now starting to punch into my back. What a sight we must have been, in this frenzied battle. Neither one of us willing to back off, each determined to come out the victor.

Those were early days before I was reigned in and subdued. Before I would quietly accept punches and slaps like they were my due. Kudos for fighting back, right? Well, the satisfaction was short lived. When the battle subsided, and all that filled the small space between us was panting and the heat of our frenzied bodies, he examined his face in the rear-view mirror and saw a tiny scratch on his nose. It was tiny, but I had drawn blood, a tiny little drop of blood, the size of a pinhead. He had to be seen in public now with this scratch, he said. His parents and people at work would see the scratch, he said. He was furious. He slapped me.

I never said a word or tried to defend myself this time. I didn't even try to block the slap. I just sat there and quietly accepted it. It was okay. I deserved it for wearing a revealing shirt and for fighting back.

'Bitch,' he spat and slapped me for the second time.

I was more worried about what I would say to my sister than I was about being assaulted, yet again, by my boyfriend.

Thankfully I could just wear the camisole. With all the calmness I could muster, I walked back to the office to start my shift that afternoon. I left my long hair loose to hide the welts and scratches on my back.

That's how the pros do it. When you're a novice, you allow the violence to play over and over in your head and affect your daily business. You cry when you're alone. You contemplate getting out, never quite sure how to do it, but knowing that if you did, it would make him sorry for being a first-class jerk. That's how it was for me when it first started.

Then, as I got accustomed to it, it just became the norm. He hit me, I cried, and I moved on. I sometimes had mere minutes in which to gather myself, banish the reality of the violence that had just happened and face colleagues or family members. I had to, because showing any trace of emotional vulnerability to family or colleagues would reveal something was wrong. And no one must ever know just how wrong things were between us. No one must and could ever know I was a victim. You stop moping around feeling sorry for yourself, you just stow away the memories of the violent confrontations and get on. You gather your breaths and slow them down to a pace that would never suggest or give away what just happened.

I had bundled up what was left of the shirt and stuffed it into my handbag before going back into the office. A few days later I was going to Johannesburg to visit my close friend Shahan Ramkissoon who worked at the SABC in Auckland Park. He didn't know I was going to visit Shahan or that I would be staying with him. I lied and told him I was going to visit a girlfriend. The torn shirt went with me on that plane to Joburg. I tossed it into a street bin while going for a walk one afternoon.

I never said a word to anyone. If Rita ever missed that shirt, she never asked or said anything. And if she had, I would have just feigned innocence and said I'd no clue what she was talking about. I had prepared an excuse, and for a long time I anticipated her suddenly asking about her shirt.

Slowly and without fanfare I came to abandon all my male friends, watched whom I spoke to at work and made sure I wasn't too friendly or smiled too much.

It's one thing limiting your exposure to men at work or in your private life, but as a journalist, being friendly is often a way to get the story. It's a key skill for the job. But he didn't seem to care if his controlling ways prevented me from doing my job properly.

I remember, for instance, how in early 2005, Schabir Shaik invited me to his house for a swim. We were at the Durban High Court, where Shaik's fraud and corruption trial was taking place. 'I don't know how to swim,' I shot back at him, to which the smooth-talking, flirtatious Shaik replied, 'That's okay, I have a lovely koi pond that you can dip your feet in.'

The next day a whole bunch of us were sitting in the SABC smoking room, when one of my colleagues who had been in court with me and within earshot of Shaik's loaded invite, recounted the exchange.

Everyone laughed, even my boyfriend. But I saw the anger dancing around his laughter, which was way too loud. I also noticed the way his eyes then clouded over, the supposed amusement in his laugh never reaching them. After that, he often came to the Durban High Court often during recesses, and I felt like he was checking up on me and my behaviour, specifically around other men.

I learnt never to be alone in the company of men, even when I was at work. I stuck to groups and mostly women. I was always on tenterhooks, never knowing when he would pitch up. I just knew I must never give him a reason to turn violent.

One day during the trial, I popped out for lunch. When I returned, another journalist sitting on the front steps of the courthouse shouted that my boyfriend had been around and was looking for me. I could see the envy in her eyes. I don't think she ever saw the terror in mine.

Even a gay friend was the subject of numerous fights between us. My gay buddy hitched a ride with me to the SABC every morning. He was still a rookie journalist then but would in time become an impossibly handsome and accomplished news anchor. He had absolutely no interest in me because he was as gay as they came.

'He's gay,' I said. 'He has no interest in me at all.' And I laughed.

It didn't matter. 'I don't care if he's a *moffie*,' he retorted. 'He's still a man. You don't need male friends. I'm the only friend you need.'

He would rub my face in his fame, flirting shamelessly with other women on and off air always, explaining it away like it was insignificant. He enjoyed the friendships of his women colleagues at Lotus FM. 'It's all part of the job,' he would say.

But it wasn't to me. It left me feeling insecure. He also often happily divulged that our colleagues asked what he was doing with me, and that exacerbated my insecurity. They wanted to know if he was desperate and couldn't do better than me, he told me, straight up.

This turned me against them. I came to despise and be very wary of nearly every single person at Lotus FM. I guess it was a way to make sure I didn't try to make friends with anyone other than him at work. My colleagues would smile and greet me in the corridors, but I knew they hated me and they mocked me behind my back, because he told me so.

Once he said one of the women presenters asked if she could introduce him to some beautiful girls, telling him that other Lotus FM staff were laughing behind his back. I was devastated. Why would she say that? What was wrong with me? I stopped speaking to her, entirely wounded and shattered. I assumed she didn't think me worthy enough, because I was dark skinned and Tamil. I had known all my life the curse of it.

I never questioned why he would tell me something so hurtful or if it was true. I never bothered to confront anyone. It didn't even occur to me that the normal thing would have been to spare me the damaging knowledge instead of telling me. Instead, I was angry and feeling particularly hateful towards pretty much everyone at Lotus FM who was supposedly ridiculing me behind my back. To me, Lotus FM became a cesspit of gossipers and people who were trying to break us up. I had no proof except what he would continuously drill into my head.

Months later I'd find a message on his phone from that same woman presenter saying she was feeling blue and wished he were there with her. When I confronted him about it, he shrugged it off, saying she probably made a mistake and sent it to the wrong person. He assured me there was nothing going on between them.

I doubted him but had to believe him. It's easier to trust a lie, especially when the truth can be crushing and destroy what you have come to believe in. Believing the lies was more for self-preservation than anything else.

I didn't want to be *that* woman, the one who was beaten and cheated on. That only happened to other women, women who had no lives, jobs or education. It didn't happen to women like me. I was on radio. I earned my own money, I could buy my own things and I had my own opinions. I was his girlfriend. From all the girls he could be with, he chose me. And they could all go jump in a lake. They would never break us up.

But on the inside, in my moments of solitude, I quietly questioned why someone like him would even want to be with me. I was ordinary, certainly no match for this fair-skinned famous guy. And so, he chiselled away at my confidence and self-esteem, and I battled to recognise it. It was subtle and clever. It fed his ego and fire, while making me feel ugly and worthless.

How do you feel anything but ugly and worthless when the man who professes to love you calls you an 'ugly black bitch'? But that was only when he was angry. When he was happy, and when I was 'good', he would tell me I was beautiful, that he loved my brown skin. That it turned him on.

Without even realising it, I was slowly changing, from my clothes to my demeanour. Changing to fit the man next to me. I was feeling foreign in my own skin but learning to embrace the conservative new version of myself. No more baring my arms in public or wearing short skirts. I was also losing friends quick and fast. The once popular girl at tech and at SABC Auckland Park was becoming a silent shadow, being pulled along by her famous boyfriend like a defeated dog. I was hardly even spending time with my family. If I weren't working, I would have to be with him. Not only did I lose so much of myself during those years, I lost valuable time with the people that mattered the most to me.

One day I got a call from Thabiso Sithole, a Joburg friend and one of my fellow SABC interns. We clicked instantly when we met then and became good buddies during the six-month internship. He was charming, funny and caring. When I was homesick, Thabiso draped his arm around my shoulders and made me laugh. Or he'd just sit and listen. He offered me a room in their home when I needed a place to stay. We were always together, inseparable at the SABC headquarters. We spent so much time together that his father – Vusi Sithole, who also worked at the SABC as a radio news editor and was kind of like my work dad – probably thought we were a couple. Thabiso later became famous as a television sports presenter at the SABC. He was always destined for greatness.

While I was thrilled to hear from Thabiso, I knew his call was going to mean trouble. And as Thabiso chatted on the other end, six hundred kilometres away, asking a million questions, eager to catch up, my body dissolved into coldness, willing Thabiso to shut up and for the call to end. Fear crept through me. My mouth was dry, my heart was racing, and I gave one-word answers. I wished I'd never answered the call, but that too would have created trouble.

We were together in the confines of his car, and it was clearly a man's voice on the other end of the line. He asked me very loudly who it was. I just looked at him and rolled my eyes in what I hoped was the best annoyed and bored look I could muster.

He was not buying my feeble attempt to show disdain. He shouted, 'You're talking to other men.'

There was a stunned silence on the other end of the line as Thabiso's voice faltered and stopped. While that call seemed to last an eternity, it ended very abruptly.

'Listen,' I said to Thabiso, 'I'm very sorry, but I can't talk to you. It's not a good time.' I cringed. Just an 'okay' from Thabiso, and the call ended.

I hoped in my heart Thabiso would know and understand it wasn't coming from the Vanessa he knew. I felt so utterly powerless in that moment and couldn't believe what I'd just done, to someone who didn't deserve it. I'd basically told my friend – someone I knew long before I met my abuser – to get lost. I'd relinquished another ounce of control over my life.

I braced myself for the punishment that was to come for even daring to talk to another man. It was ugly, and it was vile. And for all the courage of my convictions, I'm deeply ashamed to say I never did a thing to stop it. I never said a word. By not standing up, I was no better than the man who uttered these words.

I told him it was Thabiso and was busy explaining how I knew him. But he immediately flew into a rage when he heard the name Thabiso. Saliva flying from his mouth, he shouted: 'You're talking to kaffirs. My girlfriend is talking to kaffirs. Who is he to you?' He demanded to know.

And it didn't matter how much I tried to explain, he was fixated on the fact that I had been speaking to a man and, worse yet, he seemed to derive great pleasure from using the word 'kaffir' over and over again. That word was so brutal, so drenched in hate.

But I just sat there in silence and allowed him to say it. It sent torrents of hate cascading through me. A poison every bit as toxic as that word filled me up. My face and body hot with anger and fear. I died a little inside that day.

I would have preferred a slap, as it would have been less painful and traumatic. To hear that word used to describe someone I cared for and who cared for me when I struggled to settle in, during my internship in Johannesburg, shattered me.

But instead of tearing into this ranting racist fucker, I sat there, quietly waiting for his anger to subside. I dared not defend my friendship with and stand up for Thabiso.

I was afraid for myself. I was in such close proximity to a very violent man who chose to assault me with his vile racist rant rather than his fists. This was not the time to embark on a crusade to cure a bigot. No, it was a moment for self-preservation.

So, it was I who ended up apologising to him while it should have been the other way around. I will tell Thabiso never to call me again, I promised. That friendship wasn't worth our relationship, I said.

'It's you I love,' I said, hoping he couldn't hear the insincerity in my voice. Cold, rehearsed, mechanical and meaningless words to pacify the monster next to me. A necessary lie when your safety is at stake.

While he watched, I sent Thabiso a message, asking him never to call me again.

I was being denied friendship, even with old and dear friends who were in my life long before him. And so my world became smaller, revolving around him and, since we were colleagues, around work.

I was helping him with content for his solo show, coming up with ideas and writing scripts. He always picked my brain for ideas and suggestions on topics that would inspire discussion and stir controversy. I loved that everything I put together always went down well with his audience. It was sleek and sexy stuff.

I genuinely wanted success for him and for him to excel. And he did. He was brilliant at what he did. I must give him that. Radio is all about bringing in the listeners and leaving an imprint long after you have signed off. And he did that with absolute aplomb and finesse. His sexy voice sent tingles down your spine.

I was proud of our work together, and of him. But if I expected him to reciprocate, I was mistaken.

It was my ambition to read the news on radio. And soon enough, when the opportunity came, I grabbed it with both hands. Live radio thrilled me no end, and I was thriving. I lived for those days when I was scheduled to read the news on Lotus FM. I was on top of my game. I was on such a high.

But he hated my voice on radio, not for any other reason but that he felt I sounded provocative. He'd often say I sounded like I wanted to 'get fucked.' I read the news like I wanted to 'get fucked' – his words, not mine.

'One person has been shot and killed in an apparent drive-by shooting in Chatsworth just outside Durban... Two planes have ploughed into the World Trade Centre... Five people, including a six-month-old baby, have been killed in a head-on collision between a tanker and a car near Van Reenen's pass...' Gut-wrenching stuff on the news, but I sounded like I wanted to get 'fucked'.

Despite being astounded and dismayed, I managed to continue. For a while, nothing he said could quell the love and passion I had for live radio and news, not even his scathing and demeaning criticism. I think it bothered him that I held on, because he was hoping to get under my skin enough for me to fade back into the production studio and go off air.

His control over me was not yet complete. But in time, it would be.

# FOUR

# *No is not a Word I Know*

There had been another argument, and I wasn't taking any of his calls. The silent treatment was the only way of expressing my anger. I had been punished violently so many times before for giving him the silent treatment that I should have learnt my lesson. But I was obstinate even in the face of potential danger. I still hadn't mastered the art of stifling my own anger and stashing it away so that it wouldn't trigger my boyfriend's fury. Engaging with him, talking – or not – was the only thing over which I really had control. It was my only weapon. I didn't know how else to express myself other than to withdraw to a place of quiet. But my silence did nothing to douse and subdue his anger.

I was working the Saturday evening shift and read the last bulletin of the night. I was high on the rush of live radio. Sureshnie Govender, who went on to become a news anchor on 5FM, was sitting opposite me and getting ready to start her music and dedication show.

Her energy filled the studio. She was pumped up and revving to go. Our collective high from having our voices heard by thousands of people created an unspoken connection. It made us equals and made us feel powerful. It was 8pm.

As I went into the last story of the bulletin, he walked into the studio. He greeted Sureshnie, ignored me and went to stand behind her facing me. She fiddled with the sound desk, bopping her head as the music played into her earphones, oblivious to the dark aura of the man who stood behind her, arms akimbo, jaws clenched and lips pursed – all the tell-tale signs of the mounting rage that would have to erupt.

He never took his eyes off me. Not for one second. I felt his silent, savage stare burn into me as I continued to read the final story of the bulletin. I had the feeling of impending danger, of fear. If I had only known what was to come, I would have slowed down the pace, savoured every word that danced on my tongue waiting to be delivered into the microphone. I would have committed every second of that news bulletin to my memory. But we never know … until we know.

My heart raced, from the adrenaline of live radio and the dark energy that had suddenly transformed the studio. I knew every word of that 'and finally' story brought me closer to the confrontation. There would be one – of that, I was in no doubt. For a split second I probably regretted being obstinate. Why couldn't I have just swallowed my pride and kept the peace?

I wished the thousands of Lotus FM listeners goodnight, promising to catch up with them the following day and said goodbye to Sureshnie. With my heart thumping, I followed him as we walked out of the studio. My mouth was dry and my skin hot.

I had barely pulled the heavy door shut behind me when he turned and slapped me with such force that it sent me staggering backwards, pushing me into the door and flinging it open. Sureshnie looked up, stunned by the sudden interruption. He quickly pulled the door shut, pulled me by my arm and threw me against another door.

The silence was so loud, it was deafening. The air conditioner did nothing to cool down my hot skin. It took a few seconds before the studio door opened. Sureshnie stood there looking at us both. Bhangra music was blaring in the background – loud, garish and obscene in the face of my fear.

Concern was etched on Sureshnie's face. Did she know? Surely, she must have known something was wrong. 'Is everything okay?' she asked. Her eyes met mine. The question was directed at me.

I stood silently against the door. He stood a few feet away from me. My eyes looked into Sureshnie's, willing her to not close that door and leave me alone. My eyes were screaming, pleading with her to stay. Everything I couldn't say I tried to convey with my eyes.

I couldn't speak or trust myself to speak. What would I say? I was backed into a door. I was fighting back tears, terrified. Oh God, please, I silently begged, don't close that door, don't go. Don't leave me alone with him. My eyes never left hers. Why couldn't she sense what I was trying to say? I could smell myself, my fear. It filled my nostrils, almost suffocated me. Could she not smell my fear?

She stood there for what seemed like an eternity. Maybe it was only a few seconds. Then he answered, for me, his smooth, deep voice breaking the silence: 'Everything is fine. Just go back in.' Her eyes left mine and darted over to him.

As Sureshnie closed the door, my heart crumbled, my body braced itself and my mind began shutting down.

I turned to look at him. Maybe if he looked into my eyes, my face, the angry beast could be subdued. Maybe we could laugh it off. Maybe we could hold hands and walk off together and forget the slap. I would be happy to forget it, to forgive it if he would have just let it end there.

But he took a step back and raised his leg, like he was preparing to kick a ball. I didn't quite understand what was happening – until his tan Caterpillar boot ploughed into my stomach.

The sheer force of that kick sent me doubling over, currents of pain tearing through me. It felt like everything inside my stomach had been reduced to liquid. Humiliation and pain combined. But I remained on my feet, bent over, but still standing. I refused to crumble. I didn't want to fall to the floor in front of him. I clutched onto my stomach, panting, trying not to cry. It was excruciating. I didn't make a sound. Not even a whimper.

He grabbed my arm and pulled me towards the lift. My stubborn feet tried to stall, but they were two heavy slabs of concrete weighing me down. My heels dug into the carpet. Eventually I lost the battle. I could not compete with his strength and determination to drag me off somewhere quieter. Abuse needs privacy. It needs a quiet place, so that it can be exacted with fury.

I should have broken free and screamed with all my might. That would have brought the security guard, for sure. But I kept my silence.

Even now I can't answer for all the missed opportunities of drawing attention to what he was doing to me. Why I never sought police intervention – that would have been the sensible thing to do. Except, I was bound by some misguided sense of loyalty and also protecting myself from being found out. And in the Indian community, such matters should remain private.

As a journalist, I was the voice of the masses, highlighting their pain and trauma, telling their stories, which would inevitably lead to some kind of action being taken, someone coming to the rescue. But I didn't know how to speak my truth or get help for myself. I simply had no clue how to save myself.

Not a word was said between us in the elevator. There was nothing to say. He watched the numbers as the lift travelled up. I stared at the floor. I was bent over, and waves of pain flowed inside me.

There was more to come. A slap and a kick weren't enough. It was never going to be enough. I had to be taught a lesson in submission. I had to know who wielded the most power and who was ultimately in control.

Inside the main Lotus FM office, he pushed a red couch against the door to make sure no one would interrupt. Not like anyone would be coming up at that time of the night anyway. 'Sit!' he barked. And I did.

He lit a cigarette and squatted on me, his entire body weight resting on my scrawny thighs, his heavy shoes digging into me, leaving prints on my black pants. My thighs and my stomach were aching. He blew smoke into my face. He didn't say a word, just tilted his head from left to right, examining my face and blowing smoke into it. His eyes narrowed into slits. If I weren't so traumatised, I would probably have laughed at how utterly ridiculous he looked.

Tears softly and silently started streaming down my face. My self-control was diminishing with each passing second. He finished his cigarette, jumped off and ordered me to stand up.

I tried to say sorry, but he seemed unreachable. He pushed me against the wall. He took my head in both his hands and started banging it against the wall, over and over and over. Hard. Measured. Deliberate. Thud, thud, thud. Vibrations of pain were shooting through my skull. He didn't stop. He couldn't stop. He was too far gone.

I couldn't keep quiet any more. 'I am sorry,' I begged. 'Please, I am so sorry.'

I was sobbing, and all vestiges of dignity and self-control dissipated. Hot tears and snot were coursing from my eyes and nose, cascading down my cheeks, into my mouth and over my chin. I tasted salt. My hands clutched onto his, trying to still them and break the momentum of the blows.

And after what seemed like an eternity of banging my head against the wall, I saw softness and some sanity creeping into his black eyes. His hands stopped their rhythmic banging.

Still holding my head in his hands, he suddenly kissed me hard and deep. I tasted ash and emptiness. My tongue was like cardboard, dry, desolate and unwilling. But slowly I allowed my hands to reach up to hold his face, gently, and I kissed him back with what I hoped was unbridled fervour. Anything to restore calm and stop his frenzied attack. Anything.

He led me back to the red couch. He gently pushed me onto it and began unzipping his pants, his eyes boring into mine. I never took my eyes off his. I didn't want to. I couldn't.

I wanted to scream. I wanted to shout: 'I don't want this. I don't want to do this. Don't touch me with your filthy hands. I hate you.'

Instead, I allowed him to lower me onto the couch. I lay there, stiff and silent as he took off his pants. It was the grand finale of the night, the piece de résistance, the ultimate act to humiliate and subjugate.

I felt his weight on me. Still I said nothing. 'Dear God, if you are there, please help me. Make this stop,' I silently prayed. But no help came, and he didn't stop. It wouldn't be the first time that God would let me down. Where was God? Filing his fucking nails?

There was no turning back for him. My body was no longer mine. My body, my breasts, my lips, my mouth, that out-of-sight-but-never-out-of-mind place that he sought for sexual release – all belonged to him. I may have washed my body, I may have fed my body, I may have clothed my body, but my body was never truly mine.

His touch as he removed my clothes made me want to throw up. Those beautiful hands, capable of such brutality, were suddenly gentle. But the gentleness didn't mean I had any rights to my body or myself in that moment. I couldn't say no or push him away. There was no way I could say, 'Not now please.' No was not a word I knew. My mouth revolted against what my mind and brain where shouting. Pursed together, my lips were unable to say please, stop, I don't want to. I never said a word. I didn't know how to. I dared not say no.

Instead I let him do whatever he wanted.

I shivered. My teeth were chattering softly, as if I were freezing. Except it was warm inside. I was filled with such hatred and revulsion.

He stared into my eyes as he moved above and inside me; I wanted him dead. I wished he would rot in hell. The couch squeaked, seemingly protesting the despicable thing happening on it. I wanted to scream. I wanted to die. Still that couch squeaked. I wanted to claw his eyes out.

In that moment, I could understand how some women are driven to kill their abusers. I could understand the satisfaction that would come from driving a knife into the heart of someone like him.

My head throbbed. My stomach and ribs ached. His panting and moaning filled my ears and the room.

I withdrew to a place where he could never reach or hurt me. Despite what he was doing to my body, he would never get to me in that secret place deep inside my head where violent thoughts, rage, hate and fear swirled about in a tangled mess. He could harm my body, but he would never penetrate my mind and soul.

'Tell me you love me,' he whispered as he lay on top of me, still moving, his cold, empty eyes staring into mine as if he was trying to decipher me. His voice was dangerously soft and gentle.

His movements quickened. As I struggled to quell the nausea that danced in my aching stomach, my treacherous lips finally moved, uttering the words that my heart didn't feel. 'I love you,' I whispered.

Kisses and whispers can be promises of love. But they can also be cunningly deceptive, hiding fear and revulsion. It all depends on where you are, whom you are with and what it is you're hoping to achieve. Kisses and whispers are sometimes all you have to defend or protect yourself.

My stomach churned and my body rebelled as he took himself to the height of sexual release. His putrid sticky wetness trickled down my thigh, like an ashamed thing wanting to get away. It seeped into the red couch.

He stood up, zipped up his pants and walked to the toilet, leaving me alone with my humiliation and the ammoniac stench of intimacy, an assault on my nostrils, making me want to gag. I was desperate for a shower. The couch had at last gone quiet, filling the room with its sad silence.

Slowly I stood up. Standing up straight wasn't possible. The pain in my belly was still crippling. Bent over and with slow, laboured movements, I managed to pull my underwear and pants back up.

Never, not once, during that despicable act of intimacy did I let my hatred show. He would never know I didn't want to do this with him. He must never know that, because if he did, I knew it would have been the end of me.

My boyfriend had just forced himself on me for the first time. He would do it again in our years together – force himself on me. He totally disregarded me and had contempt for my feelings, for not wanting to be intimate.

It feels strange to use the word 'rape', as it's hard to think of sexual assault – against one's will – happening between lovers. Some part of me believed that in choosing to be with him, I was consenting to anything and everything in our relationship, even sex when I didn't want to. I had covered many stories of rape and women's rights issues, but that was the rule I applied to my relationship and myself; I was his girlfriend, so no consent was required. How could this be rape? But spousal or intimate partner sexual assault is a thing. It's real.

One time I did tell him I really wasn't up to it and that I didn't want to be intimate after an argument. He slapped me hard and accused me of being unfaithful. 'If you don't want to do this with me, then who are you screwing?' he asked. 'No one,' I responded, kissed him and again allowed him to do what he wanted.

The body becomes a weapon in the battle for power and peace. That space between a woman's legs can be a curse or a blessing depending on the moment and the emotion. It can know greatness, such as when a baby passes through; and it can suffer the worst defilement. Not even the girl baby, the threat of that place between her legs barely even formed, is spared. Neither is the wise old woman, fragile and wilted by her years. The space between a woman's legs can be her power or her poison.

Even when I told him I was having my period, it did nothing to quell his desire, despite his religion forbidding intercourse during menstruation. The first time I tried to use my period to stave him off, he pulled down my pants and underwear, and my drenched sanitary pad fell to the ground, my face burning with humiliation as I scrambled to pick it up and hide it from his eyes. Even in the midst of that violent moment of intimacy I tried valiantly to cling to my dignity, a bloodied pad on the floor. But we were lovers. I was his girlfriend. Nothing was sacrosanct.

Following the assault in the studio, I suffered for days, not able to walk up straight. I started convincing myself I'd asked for it. I should have known not to ignore him. I should have known better than to start a fight.

I would never win!

I wonder if that red couch is still there in the Lotus FM office. How many people have sat on that couch, laughing, talking and eating? That silent, inanimate witness. An unassuming, slightly battered red couch, the only witness to the night I forced myself to lie down, patiently masking all my contempt and disgust for the man who laboured above and in me. That red couch – the only witness to my subjugation.

The only witness to my rape.

# FIVE

# The Price of Silence and the Cost of Defiance

Being forced to be intimate straight after being kicked in the stomach by my lover was actually a small price to pay for my silence and defiance. There was a bigger cost than having my body and soul violated, I would find out in the days following that awful night that ended on the red couch.

After that night, I was never the same again. He had altered me profoundly. With his hands, his tan Caterpillar-clad foot, the banging of my head against the wall and, finally, the unzipping of his pants, he altered me forever. With each of those acts, he stripped me of the last remaining bits of my confidence and seamlessly instilled fear of catastrophic proportions.

Never again would I be able to read news live on radio without being struck by debilitating and uncontrolled panic attacks. Every time I switched on the microphone and the red on-air light came on, an overwhelming fear filled me. It would surround the air around me, enveloping me in its dark thickness, and fill up my senses, wrapping its unseen fingers around my throat and brain and leaving me feeling completely desolate and destroyed. I couldn't breathe. I felt like I was suffocating. Words would stay stuck inside my mouth, wrapped around my tongue, unable and unwilling to come out of my mouth. My throat narrowed, not leaving enough space for air. I was constantly swallowing saliva in between words to get air into my body and the words out. The panic attacks just grew worse with every passing day and every bulletin I read.

It was the one thing that was left that brought me profound joy and fulfilment, and it would become the thing to torment me and throw me into turmoil.

Being a news anchor required sitting down, plucking up the courage, controlling your nerves and reading your stories, every hour on the hour. That was my job and I revelled in it. I lived for those three to four minutes every hour when I would read the news live. The timbre in my voice rising and falling, the dramatic pauses. I was the deliverer of tragedies and triumphs.

Of what use is a newsreader that can't get the words out of their mouth?

I became so afraid of live radio that I eventually asked my editor to be taken off air. I was taken off air and was lucky that I didn't lose my job. What I did lose, though, was something far more valuable and irreplaceable – my dignity and reputation as a newsreader.

I didn't keep it secret that I asked to be taken off because I suffered panic attacks. There were whispers and smug looks but enduring these was still better than the trauma of trying to get through a bulletin on air.

Broadcast journalism is cutthroat. There's always someone waiting in the shadows, greedy to take your place, hear their voice on air and have their moment of glory. There are very few real friends when you're in radio or television. So, when my time as a newsreader ended abruptly, many were thrilled, secretly or not so secretly pleased that I'd made way for them to shine.

I was the girl who starred in school plays. The one who was called to do book reviews in front of the whole school. I excelled at speeches. It was my thing. It was the one thing I was so good at without even having to try.

Growing up, I dreamt of becoming a news anchor on TV or radio. I never thought the daughter of a truck driver could do that. Radio and television seemed unreachable for the child of uneducated, poor parents. And for a brief time, I was doing the thing I dreamt of. Forget a few hundred kids at the school assembly, I was now informing thousands across the country.

And now the thing I loved so much was an endless source of trauma. I just could not manage the panic attacks.

My editor, Ami Nanackchand, let me off the hook. No questions asked. Even with that I was lucky. I wasn't sacked, admonished or humiliated. Ami just quietly accepted that I no longer wanted to read the news and was no longer capable to do so. Even through all the misery, there were moments of luck when I got away easily. Just never with my boyfriend though.

It would be at least two years before I would get back into live radio and try and reclaim my career. Two years before I could face my fears.

I started with a baby step, not with a newscast but with a sports bulletin on Newsbreak, a morning show. It was a very early show, and I was hoping there wouldn't be too many people listening at that time. I was so terrified that I gave the anchor, Aasra Bramdeo, copies of all the stories I had to read. If I faltered and couldn't go on, she would immediately pick up and continue.

This was live radio, on a national station with a few thousand people listening. And there I was, facing my demons with the help of a consummate and respected professional to be my back-up should I fail. This was unheard of, probably even highly unprofessional on my part.

Aasra took the copies from me, silently pledging her support. I have known cruelty and terror. But I have also known such kindness and compassion.

I clawed my way back to live radio. But it was never quite the same. There would never be any enjoyment or satisfaction, just a quiet sense of accomplishment every time I managed to do a news bulletin without falling apart at the seams.

I also clung to any kind of acknowledgement of my work in those days. I remember reading the 7am bulletin one morning shortly after venturing back on air and sitting at my desk trying to still my racing heart and come to terms with what I felt was an enormous accomplishment. Ami, perhaps, realising this said, 'I'm so proud of you,' as he strolled past my desk. No good morning or how are you – just those sparing and beautiful words handed delicately to me.

But I took every step to ensure my reading the news would never be cause for consternation to him or me. I avoided direct contact with the DJs, who were mostly men, by reading the news from the production studio instead of the live studio. I couldn't bear being inside that studio anyway without feeling trapped and scared.

But even though I managed to avoid the live studio where it all started that night, the fear was always there, taunting me and making sure I remained its slave. A cruel reminder of what I allowed to happen to me, over and over.

Even when I was already with e.tv, live crossings from the field were an endless source of stress. I'd spend hours staring into the mirror, looking deep into my own eyes and talking to the person inside, convincing her there was nothing to be afraid of, whispering the mantra I created and recited every single time before reading news on Lotus FM: 'You can do this, Vanessa. You have done this before. Just stay calm. Breathe. Enjoy it. This is what you were born to do. This is what you have always wanted to do. It's okay to feel nervous. It is okay to feel anxious. But there is nothing to be afraid of. I am sorry for all the bad things that I let happen to you. I am sorry that you had to go through what you went through. But that is never going to happen to you again. I will never let that happen to you ever again. He can never hurt you. You are Vanessa Govender... No one is going to take that away from you. Just do it.'

That mantra would still my racing heart and pacify and soothe my raging head.

Should I blame him or myself for this?

I always held onto the belief that he robbed me of my career on radio. He stole my confidence and reduced me to nothing.

But then again, it was I who let him. It was I who opened the door to his brand of evil and stoked the flames of his rage. I allowed it to happen to me.

# SIX

# *Tangled Webs*

Apart of why I allowed it to happen and stuck with him was because this famous man chose to be with me. He told me no man would ever want or love me the way he did.

When you grow up being teased and taunted by kids at school for being dark skinned, I guess you become a sucker for the first person who casually tosses a few flattering words or attention your way – especially when that someone is a high-flying, smooth-talking celebrity. The world wants him, but it's *you* he's chosen.

He reeled me in, and before long his kind looks and carefully crafted, charming words morphed into something nasty and vicious before becoming entrenched in my head. Every time I thought to leave – and whenever I tried – I heard those words, telling me that there would be no one else, and they would lure me back into his arms.

Because who would or could love someone like me, the dark-skinned girl? I carried that from childhood into adulthood, the shameful burden of being my shade of brown. My schoolmates ridiculed me because of my skin colour. From as young as five I endured the taunts.

Blackie! Black thing! Ugly black dog!

A primary school friend confessed many years later that her mother forbade her from playing with me because of my dark skin. She was my best friend at the time, and I could never understand why she no longer wanted to play with me. I'd done nothing. I was shattered. I was only six years old, and my heart was broken because my best friend had dumped me for no apparent reason.

The bullying and ridiculing continued in high school. In Standard 7 the boy I sat next to in science class once, totally out of the blue, asked, 'Why are you so black and ugly?' I laughed, summoning up the best, 'Oh, you're so lame' look and carried on with my work, fighting back the tears. I wanted to run out of that classroom and away. Inside I just wanted to die.

I grew up during apartheid in the 1970s and '80s. I didn't understand much about it and was unaware that the colour of my skin meant there were places I couldn't go, places I couldn't sit, toilets I couldn't use. I knew nothing of this kind of discrimination. No, the only prejudice I endured because of my skin colour was from my own people.

I had no concept of racism, but I understood colourism in all its infinite ugliness and cruelty without knowing what it was called. Carried here by the indentured labourers and passed down through the generations, it is the legacy of India's caste system, under which so-called *dalits* or untouchables are ostracised because of their dark skin and social standing.

Within the Indian community, lighter-skinned people are often considered attractive – and better – than everyone else. It doesn't matter if you barely scrape through school or if you're not that easy on the eye, but fair skin gets you respect and admiration. The teachers favour you, family and friends treat you like royalty. You just have a better life. You're seen as a suitable partner. Not all Indian people think this way, but many do. There's this obsession about being fair.

Even among the dark skinned there is a hierarchy of brownness.

Some dark-skinned people discriminate against people who are a shade or two darker – and there is always someone darker. Being mocked by others doesn't stop the person suffering the prejudice from dishing out his or her own disdain and contempt.

My heart aches when I see a dark-skinned child, because I know what is in store for him or her. I sometimes feel like all I want to do is bundle that child in my arms and whisper: 'You're beautiful. Never let anyone define your beauty and your worth by this skin you're in. You are so much more than your skin too. One day, someone somewhere is going to look at you and think how utterly beautiful you are … Because of that rich coffee colour.' But I can't and I won't. They will figure out the might of their shade in time, and when they do, it will be such a revelation.

We pass it down to our children, and they pass it down to theirs. And on and on it goes; we are ugly and worthless because of our shade of brown. We are nothing, we have no feelings, we don't get wounded when you shun us. We are dark skinned, we are dirt, we must accept the scorn because it is our lot in life.

Sometimes when people, especially relatives, wanted to be kind they told me, 'You're pretty, even though you are dark.' Or, 'You may be dark, but you have nice features.' I think they meant those comments to be compliments. But what the fuck did that mean? A family friend once said to my mother, 'If Vanessa was fair, she would be even more pretty.' She was an educated woman. A teacher.

It must be a wonderful thing to be fair, I believed growing up. I could deal with not being the smartest kid or with being poor. But being dark was a life sentence.

Even newborn babies aren't exempt. A little baby whose journey in this world is only just beginning is still oblivious to the curse, the whispers and comments that are tossed about recklessly: 'Shame, the baby is a bit dark.' The poor child is doomed by no choice of its own and without them knowing it. But before long, though, they realise.

It's a life sentence of being mocked and ridiculed. It's a lifetime of never being enough or worthy. You work extra hard at being likeable, funny, clever, just so no one notices the dark skin too much.

Being dark skinned was crushing. It tore me to shreds, those taunts, yelled out loud enough for everyone on the playground or in the classroom to hear. Other kids would laugh. I would too, just to show I didn't care, that it didn't bother me at all. Inside I was dying. I hated myself. I hated my parents for bringing me into this world, and I hated my dirty skin. I was just a child.

It was relentless. I prayed for my life to end. I even sometimes prayed to God to make me lighter skinned. I could not bear to even look at myself in the mirror sometimes. I despised what I saw. I would scrub my skin raw in the bath, in the hope of washing the darkness away. It refused to budge. I was stuck with it.

I was ten years old the first time I tried to end my life. Just ten years old, I was already sick and tired of being alive, of being mocked and stuck in my dark skin. I had a bath, swallowed a handful of my mother's sleeping pills and went to bed hoping to never wake up again. But I did, groggy and out of it. I don't think anyone ever knew or suspected a thing.

I guess I had been courting death before I even understood its absolute finality. Anything to not feel the pain and anguish of being trapped in the uncompromising and unforgiving coffee colour of my skin.

My mother is dark skinned, and my father was lighter. Rita and Preshene took after him. In our home, and with our varying hues of brown, skin colour was never an issue. We were all what we were. My parents never made me feel anything but loved and would tell me often I was pretty, but still I envied my sisters for their light complexion and wished that I had inherited that from my dad too.

My mother always told me how my dad told her how beautiful she was. Like me, she too had endured taunts as a child and was very sensitive about being dark. My father always told her that she was a beautiful woman, and he admired her.

She would tell me this and often recount how they met. My father was actually supposed to marry Aunt Sally, my mom's older sister. The day he arrived with my granny Allimah Govender, his mother, to propose to Aunt Sally, my mother caught his eye instead. She was the younger and darker-skinned one, shyly loitering in the background, and she won the heart of the handsome Frank Govender that day. Whenever my mother tells her love story, you see the memory softening the lines on her face. But it didn't make me feel better about myself.

I didn't confide in her that I was being teased and bullied. Walking back from school, I would often be ridiculed by a band of boys, their ring leader a horrid boy who lived up the road from us who yelled 'Blackie' at me over and over making me cry all the way home. But I always dried my tears and changed my demeanour before walking through the door. I was too embarrassed for my mother or sisters to know what was happening. I was just a child, but even then, I knew how to lie and put on a brave face.

Plus, if my mother found out she would probably have gone banging on the doors of those boys' homes to tell their parents what she thought of their bratty little sons. So, I kept the secret partly because of embarrassment and largely because of fear for my mother's over protectiveness, which would just make the situation worse. I went to school every day and accepted the bullying. It was just the order of things in our little Indian community. If you're dark skinned, don't expect to slip under the radar.

It was only in my thirties and long after he was out of my life that I came to realise one very simple but very powerful fact. I'm pretty *because* I'm dark. I finally came to love the skin I was born in. And it was people from other race groups and different parts of the world who opened my eyes and my heart to liking myself and the way I looked.

I couldn't bear for another child to endure what I did, so I wrote a long Facebook post about the issue of skin colour within the Indian community. At the time, 'Unfair and Lovely' and 'Dark is Beautiful' campaigns were sweeping through Bollywood. The stunning actress Nandita Das, who had been the victim of her own skin tone, was the poster girl for these campaigns. I knew it was time for frankness and brutal honesty. It was time for South Africans Indians to be called out for their deplorable discrimination. I was no longer ashamed to admit I was a victim of colourism.

*'Let's have this conversation!' I wrote. 'People are quick to vent and get angry over racist comments and behaviour, yet racist attitudes are very prevalent within particular race groups. I speak from and about my personal experience within my own community. Growing up I was often taunted and teased for being dark skinned, so much so that I was angry with my parents for bringing me into this world. Kids at primary school made my life a hell because of my dark skin. There were times I even wanted to end my life because of the colour of my skin and how others made me feel about it. It was so bad.*

*'Yes, I accept that it is your own reaction to what people say and do that defines what you feel inside. But to a ten-year-old child that kind of hindsight doesn't exist.*

*'I was robbed of that carefree existence and a constant dark shadow followed me. It took travelling and a job on television to finally alter my own feelings towards myself and the skin I was born in.*

*'From Bangkok to London, Paris to Sudan, wherever I would go, people would stop and stare, smile and ask my name. People wanted to know me.*

*'At first, I felt conspicuous and then it slowly began to dawn on me, a beautiful revelation. It was nothing short of a rebirth.*

*'I started feeling whole and peace began to settle in the deepest corners of my mind and heart. Those very places that once harboured insecurity and self-hate.*

*'Men and women smiled, and, in their eyes, I could read the*

*acknowledgement and appreciation for the person who stood in front of them or passed them on the streets.*

*'And it dawned on me that the very thing that once brought me shame was in fact the thing that made me beautiful, sultry, seductive and sought after.*

*'If you were to ask me what the most attractive or sexiest part of me is, without hesitation I would answer: my dark skin.*

*'Some people spend a fortune trying to imitate it. Others spend their money trying to chase the lighter side of their complexion and that for me is tragic, because beneath the pursuit of fairness probably lies a lifetime of rejection and humiliation – and the misguided notion that dark equals ugly.*

*'Colour is an issue in the Indian community – always has been.*

*'We hide behind this veneer of propriety and integrity when the bitter reality is that most people are caught in this warped perception that fair skin is beautiful and dark skin is something to be ashamed of.*

*'Ironically, one of my tormentors professed love when I was about 19, after making my life a misery throughout primary school.*

*'The colour of my skin was still the same. It hadn't altered one least bit.*

*'I rose above the labels, I rose above the cruel taunts, not because of inner strength but because of one simple revelation: the greater majority of people in this world don't care about it.*

*'Where are all the people who thought it was fun to mock me? Somewhere, lost in obscurity.*

*'I love my brown skin. Today I wear it with pride and confidence.*

*'People within the Indian community who still feel fair-skinned or light-skinned people are more attractive have clearly never been anywhere beyond the confines of their homes and their minds.*

*'I am and always will be the last person to ever judge anyone based on skin colour. I would rather die first than ever wound anyone with cruel words about it.*

*'I urge children and people who have endured similar heartache to take a good look at themselves... Celebrate the skin you are born in.*

*'The richness of your brownness is beautiful.*

*'Take it from me.'*

*Post*, a newspaper serving the Indian community, picked up on what I'd written on Facebook and asked if they could publish it. I didn't think twice. The more people this reached, the better. If I could show people I wasn't embarrassed to own what happened to me and speak my truth, it would hopefully make a difference in someone else's life. Early in 2016, the article appeared on the second page and was titled 'Brownness is Beautiful'.

But it has been a long journey to make peace with my skin colour. Back then, I thought I was nothing special. I never believed I was. My time at the Technikon and the internship at the SABC gave me a small ego boost. But I was still always aware. The taunts and teasing never strayed too far from my memory. They were always there to remind me of who and what I really was.

I don't know if that's the reason I never actually went for any of the guys who asked me out at tech, or the dishy 5FM DJ who openly flirted with me whenever I walked past the studio in Auckland Park as an intern. Maybe I was secretly afraid it was all some horrid joke. I was shy and unsure of myself and why any guy would pay me attention. I'd look at my hands or stare at my face in the mirror – nothing exceptional, nothing special. I couldn't see past the colour of my skin.

So, you can imagine when this popular tall, fair-skinned DJ kept checking me out and eventually made me his girlfriend, I was already primed and easy picking for any bit of affection. I was moulded, shaped and defined for the role of the abused woman. Even though I cowered in his shadow, I was still someone he chose to be with, despite the colour of my skin.

But here's the thing, he was equally prejudiced about skin colour. At one point he regularly co-hosted a show with a woman who was also dark skinned. And while they seemed to get on, he would often say vicious things about her skin colour behind her back. He'd call her an 'ugly black thing' and say only 'desperate men' wanted to be with her. Knowing she and I had the same burden to bear, this just further fuelled my own insecurity, of course.

From his mean words, he seemed to despise her. Why, then, was I so suspicious of them together? There was that one time when they were talking live on air about pet names and terms of endearments people reserved for their other halves. They were calling each other these names in soft, flirtatious voices dripping with sexiness and laced with promises. Well, that's how it sounded to my ears. I was listening in from the newsroom while I was compiling the next bulletin. I understand the concept of radio and that banter is necessary to spice up the airwaves and keep listeners guessing. I got that it was a show, but it sounded pretty real to me.

Maybe I felt jealous because she was there with him and I was unable to be on air because of my anxiety. Or maybe I was downright angry about his double standards. I couldn't talk to any men, even my colleagues, without it escalating to a violent confrontation between us. Whatever it was, I could feel the anger welling up in me as I listened to them on radio.

I headed to the studio to drop off the bulletin with the newsreader. What I saw turned my already boiling blood into a raging river of lava. There they sat, opposite each other, the normally bright lights dimmed, busy crooning pet names to each other on live radio. Why turn the lights down low?

I dropped off the bulletin and went back upstairs. But there was no way I would be letting this one go. After his show I met him outside the studio. The air between us was thick. I could feel my breath, hot and fast. My head was spinning, and my mouth was dry, my tongue thick in anticipation of the angry words that would come spewing out. I wasn't afraid of the consequences. I didn't even stop to think about them. I was seething.

We headed off to a small hidden spot at the end of the corridor. No sooner had we reached its sanctuary than the bitter accusations started flying from my mouth. I felt betrayed, hurt, insecure and angry by the things he said on air and by the fact that the two of them sat huddled together in the dark like lovers. It was intimate and crossed the boundaries of professionalism. I told him all these things.

'How could you?' I spat. 'If that were me in there you would rip me to shreds.'

It was inappropriate, I told him. I would never dare do something like that.

I never got too far with my tirade. Midway through, his fist slammed into my face, connecting with my nose and sent me staggering backwards. I saw the proverbial stars, tiny little spots of light. My head snapped back. My ears were ringing. My face was on fire. My nose throbbed. The pain was unbelievable.

Within seconds, even before he drew his fist back from my face, I felt the warm blood cascade from inside my nose. It tasted coppery and smelled sickeningly sweet. I ran to the nearest toilet, leaving a trail of blood all over the carpet. The SABC corridors were quiet. It was always my crappy luck.

Inside the toilet, the sterile white tiles soon resembled a garish hospital theatre room from hell. There was blood everywhere. I couldn't stop the bleeding. I locked myself in a cubicle, desperately stuffing toilet paper into my nose. I didn't realise he had followed me into the toilet until I heard him speak. He was in the cubicle next door, standing on the toilet seat, smoking and peering at me.

'Why do you always have to cause problems? Look at what you have done.' He spoke in a very calm, measured voice.

I couldn't believe what I was hearing, that he was accusing me of causing problems. I was still in shock from the punch and the blood pouring out of my nose, so I didn't respond.

The toilet floors were a mess. I tried my best to clean them up, but it still looked gross in there. He kept talking. The stench of the blood and cigarette smoke was a sickening combination. I would often be reminded of this incident when, as a television news reporter, I arrived at a crime or accident scene and there was death and destruction all around me. In an instant, these scenes would catapult me back in time to that toilet, to that afternoon. The smell of blood would for many years conjure up that violent encounter.

My anger was subsiding. There was no room for anger when I was in such pain. I had a pounding headache and my nose, God, my nose hurt. There was a tiny cut where my skin split on the bridge of my nose, barely visible unless you cared to look. Weeks later it was the only visible evidence that would remain of what had happened that afternoon.

We walked out of that bathroom, my nose stuffed with the cheap, single-ply toilet paper. I was subdued and already concocting my lie. He was still harping on about me always wanting to cause problems and driving him to hit me because he felt cornered and didn't know how else to get through to me.

'I can't reach you when you're like that,' he said. 'I love you, and it drives me insane that you don't seem to get that through your thick head.'

I struggled to make sense of his love – ardent, full of sound and fury – but, like Shakespeare said of life, signifying nothing.

My father was waiting outside in the visitors' parking to fetch me from work. We said our goodbyes, terse and tense. Heck, I even got a parting kiss.

I explained what had happened to my dad, who looked startled to see me in the dim interior light of the car, which came on the moment I opened the door. I was still clutching my nose. I was bending down to pick up some papers, and someone opened the studio door just as I was standing up. The door hit me in the face, I told my dad. No big deal,

I said. There was just a little nosebleed and a small cut where the door handle struck my nose.

My father being my father didn't say too much, except that he would take me straight to Preshene's surgery to have it checked out. Both my sisters are doctors. I repeated my story to Preshene.

The stories I came up with were creative, and I could come up with them in a couple of seconds flat. Sometimes he would have me run those lies by him first. That night no one asked too many questions because no one had any reason to suspect anything dark and dangerous was going on and that the outspoken, sassy and bossy Vanessa was being beaten up by her boyfriend.

The next day at work, a story was doing the rounds that someone had a miscarriage in the women's bathroom near the live studios. I listened to the gossip with what I hope was disbelief etched on my face. Perhaps it was genuine disbelief. I didn't quite realise how much I'd bled.

As long as they all were buying into that story, I didn't have to worry about coming up with any more lies.

As for us, a quiet camaraderie prevailed. We were laughing and joking again soon enough, the events of the night before a shameful secret quickly stashed away. Maybe I did get some sense punched into me after all, I thought. I must have been silly to make a big deal of the studio flirting. He was with me. He had chosen to be with me.

I might have prided myself on my storytelling abilities, but I didn't fool everyone. Some weeks later, while I was putting on make-up, my mother asked if he was hitting me. 'No,' I said, without missing a beat. With a steady hand, I continued to do my make-up. 'He would never hurt me.'

I asked where she got that ridiculous idea. Someone called her and told her he was abusive and doing drugs. 'Is it true?' she asked again.

I had a chance to come clean, to share the secrets that weighed so heavily on me. For a few seconds I toyed with the idea. I could almost feel that liberation that comes with unburdening oneself. I craved it. And more than that, I yearned for someone to save me.

But instead, I laughed at her. 'That's ridiculous,' I said. 'People are jealous of our relationship.' She was quiet after that, but she knew. And she was not the only one in the family.

One morning in 2003, Rita walked into my bedroom to say hello. I sat up in bed. I was still drowsy, my mouth thick with sleep, my brain and thoughts still gathering themselves to face another day.

I swallowed, and it hurt like hell. My throat was sore, and my neck ached. We had fought the day before. I had ruined the fragile peace again. Somewhere along the line he wound his hands so tightly around my neck that I thought I was going to pass out.

I remember gasping for air and feeling blackness sweeping over me, as I clutched onto his hands and clawed at his fingers, trying to loosen the grip. I tried to gulp down what little air I could manage but nothing was coming through. My head felt like it was going to explode from the mounting pressure of not having enough air. He was killing me, his fuming face inches from mine. He was taking my life.

I couldn't even plead or say sorry, because I couldn't breathe. I could hear my own desperate rasping as I gasped. No air was going down. There was not an inch of space for even a wisp of air to slip through. His beautiful fingers had made sure of it. I was barely able to stand as he slowly tightened his grip. My legs buckled. He seemed to take immense pleasure as I struggled and flayed in front of him. My body was desperately trying to cling to consciousness, maybe even life, even though I actually wanted neither. Even though I had been seeking death all my life, my treacherous body was fighting to stay alive.

And just before I could pass out, seconds from that deliciousness of shutting down and not knowing and feeling anymore, he stopped. He had no intention of killing me. He was just making a point. Teaching me a lesson.

Bent over, I greedily gulped down air, choking on it. I could not get enough air in to get words out. I could feel the dampness of my underwear and got the whiff of urine. I had peed in my pants as he throttled me.

I managed an apology. My voice barely a whisper, it shivered, and it shook. It took every ounce of physical strength to bring my body back from that place his choking fingers were dragging me to. The apology was important. It was my white flag for us to reach a temporary truce.

Lesson learnt!

The angry blue fingerprints he left spoke for themselves and would last for days. I'd usually be careful and cover them up with my long hair, but Rita caught me off guard, just as I woke up. She stopped in her tracks and broke off talking in the middle of her sentence. Her eyes fell to my neck. I felt the heat and humiliation creep up and wash over my face as the realisation of what she was looking at dawned on me. Shit, I had forgotten.

'What's that? What happened?' she asked, pointing at my neck. Her usually calm and content face became distraught at first – and then angry.

I sat there numb with silence, trying to shake off the remnants of sleep, and will my weary body and mind to snap out of its defeated reverie. I was unable to prise anything from my usually enterprising and scheming head.

The imprints of his fingers and my forgetfulness to cover his tracks would expose us both and bring every lie and truth spilling out, tangled together, and desperate for acknowledgment and release. I stared at Rita, in the soft glow of the morning sunlight that streamed through my bedroom window, unable to speak.

Tears trickled down her face. And so, I wept too. I cried with my sister. I cried because she cried for me. I cried for her, and I cried for me. I cried for every single time I had ever been hit and had to hide it. I cried because I couldn't understand how one human being could do all the things he did to another human. I cried because it was happening to me.

I cried also perhaps not just because of the physical pain or the humiliation or the lies I had told to cover it up. I think I also cried more out of fear that this would spell the end of the relationship.

I wanted it to be over, so why was I scared now that the truth was out? I'd been found out. No one in my family would allow the relationship to continue. But he would never let me go. He told me so.

Rita walked out without saying another word and told my parents. I didn't tell them about the countless times he had hit me. I didn't tell them about each incident. I didn't even have to admit or confess to him hitting me. The marks around my neck spoke for themselves and confirmed their suspicions. They didn't ask too much, and I didn't say too much. There was really nothing to be said.

But now they knew. And whether it had only been that one time or hundreds of other times was irrelevant. Once was more than enough for them. My parents and sisters each took turns to talk to me, reach out and plead with me to leave. They forbade me from seeing him again.

I sent him an SMS telling him they found out and didn't want me seeing him anymore. It wouldn't be easy. We worked in the same building. And, besides, leaving him was not an option.

I went to work and returned later, tired and enveloped in sadness. That evening, after my tangled web of lies came undone, will forever remain etched in my mind, stamped into my soul. Even now, I close my eyes and go back to that night. I was sitting at the dining table, eating supper by myself. My father came to sit with me at the table.

He was a man who never said too much and never interfered. There he was, the silent and patient parent, reaching out to me. Gently pleading, he said, 'Please leave him, because if you ever marry this man there is nothing I can do to help you.'

My father never dictated to us how to live or scolded or yelled at my sisters and me. It was my mother who was the disciplinarian. My father read his newspaper from cover to cover, watched the news on television, and if I ever asked his permission, he directed me to my mother, whose decision was final. Even when my dad found out that I was dating someone who was not Hindu, he just quietly said if that's what made me happy, then that's all there was to it. And there he was, begging me. In that moment, when he should have been in a rage, he remained calm, his tired face, which bore the traces of the illness that plagued him pretty much his entire adult life, looked pained and in turmoil. He suddenly looked old and tired. Did I not notice this before?

His words entered my ears and stayed stuck in my head. Those words will never leave me. He had barely finished talking when I started sobbing, loudly and without shame. Tears ran down my face, dripping onto my plate. There was a lead ball stuck in my throat. My hunger had been replaced by defeat and self-pity.

'I can't.' I cried. 'I can't leave him.' No reason given.

None asked. Quietly, my father just stood up and walked away. My saviour, my life-giver walked away. I defied him, the man who wanted my safety and happiness. I defied my father and chose instead the man who said he loved me so much that I drove him to dangerous displays of affection: punches, slaps, kicks – and even rape.

Defying my father torments me still. It's soul crushing. And it's something I must live with every day of my life. How must he have felt in that instant, when I made my choice? I never stopped to consider him or any of my family. It must have been awful for them every time I drove off with him, as they no doubt feared that it might be the last time they'd see me, that he would kill me.

I couldn't finish my food that night. It hurt to swallow. I took a hot bath and went to bed. I was 26, but I felt old and tired. My friends were out partying and having fun. And here I was – too afraid to break up with my abusive boyfriend.

Rita still hoped to convince me to leave him. She asked Dr Nadine Rapiti, one of her colleagues, to try and talk some sense into me. The three of us met one evening in the foyer of the SABC building where I worked. In a gentle voice, Nadine, whom I barely knew, told me what I already knew but refused to acknowledge. Rita sat there, crying for most of the time. Sadness and frustration seemed to flow down her face. I think she realised it was a losing battle. I was resigned to my decision.

So my family said they wanted to speak to him. He came to our home a few days later. He would be the peacemaker this time and make my family forgive him and welcome him back. Him and I sat together on one couch in the lounge of our family home, holding hands – my allegiance was clear. I had picked a side.

My parents, Rita and Selvan, her husband, could have been visitors in their own home as they took their seats. He apologised. He did at least have the courage and was honest enough to admit to being abusive. He said he would never do it again and explained that I would push him to a point of no return. I was obstinate and always accusing him of messing around with other girls. I didn't understand that radio meant he had a lot of fans, mostly women, and that he would have to interact with them, but they meant nothing. I couldn't get that, he told them, and it was always the root cause of all the problems in our relationship.

The truth is I was always insecure, feeling like I was competing with hundreds of other girls. I was afraid he would find someone prettier; scared he would come to his senses. It's true all the things he said to them that night in our lounge.

But did he have to hit me for it? Did he have to punch me? Did he have to kick me? Did he have to add to my insecurities by feeding it with his stories and bragging about the droves of women and their indecent proposals?

He told my family that I provoked all the beatings. I drove him to it, and out of sheer frustration, he would resort to hitting me because he didn't know how else to get through to me.

Rita and Selvan told him it was utter rubbish, a feeble excuse. Walk away if you feel angry, they said, but you should never raise a hand to her.

He looked my father in the face and apologised. He promised he would never do it again and charmingly assured them he was madly in love with me, and I meant the world to him. Even when my father should have been in a rage, he remained dignified and gave him the benefit of the doubt, showing him the courtesy he really didn't deserve. Looking back I think this display from my father was not weakness but a show of absolute fortitude so as not to alienate a child who had already decided to take the side of her tormentor. What do you do as a parent so as to keep your child safely within reach and not push them away in attempting to actually keep them safe?

I could almost forgive him for all the terrible things he did to me. But coming into my father's home that night and lying to his face – that's unforgiveable. It was by far the biggest sin he would and could commit.

He was good. He could charm anyone. I could see his appeal and understand how people were drawn to him. He was on radio, and fame makes you appealing, but he had more than just fame. He had charisma. He could get most people eating out of his hand and buying into whatever it was he said or did. And so it was that my family bought into the apology and promise he made in my father's house in late 2003.

He did stop, for a while at least.

In the months following that family intervention, however, something slowly started unfolding within the confines and sanctuary of our home. By December that year, I would learn a brutal lesson in life, love and loss.

# SEVEN

# When Death Comes Calling and the Tin House of Dreams

I grew up in a two-roomed tin house in an area called Mayville near Cato Manor in Durban. I'm being quite generous in calling it a house. It wasn't a home that gave us dignity; it was a place to cook and sleep. Space was a luxury that poor people had absolutely no concept of.

Summers were cruel; the heat and humidity were exacerbated by our cramped living conditions. Winters were unforgiving, as the chill would snake its way in through the cement floors and the walls of our threadbare tin home and we'd struggle to warm up. The kids slept on the floor, and I remember the cold seeping up into my skin and bones and us drawing closer together, tighter to steal warmth from each other. It's perhaps the hardships we endured together in that tiny tin house that sealed the impenetrable bonds between Rita, Preshene and me, and led to our dreams for more.

We didn't have much, but I didn't know that back then. To my little girl eyes and mind, we had it all. My father, his brothers and their children all lived together on the same property. There was our little turquoise tin house and another main building that had a few rooms, one per family. Each of us as poor as the next.

We huddled around the fire on winter evenings and waited patiently for huge drums of water to heat up, so we could bathe. We watched the flames dance and felt the chill. The older kids would tell stories, fireflies adding to the magic.

Long summer days were spent playing with makeshift toys. What we lacked in money, we made up for with our ingenuity. We nailed pieces of wood together, and sticks, stones and other scrap we could find became whatever our imagination could conceive.

There were trees to climb, a wide expanse of a vegetable garden to explore and in which to while away the hours. My sisters sang to me and concocted wonderful stories of monsters and trolls that filled my ears, terrifying and exhilarating me and eventually carrying me to sleep.

My only source of fear and consternation was our pit toilet outside, a few metres from the house. I was petrified I would fall in and that it would be the end of me. And it reeked. But I learnt to hold my nose and face my fears. Heaven forbid you needed to use the toilet at night. There were no lights and you had to take a torch with you and walk in absolute darkness, the smell guiding you to its murky depths and its promise of relief.

At three and four years old, despite the dangers of the pit latrine, life was simple, easy and beautiful.

Ten years my senior, Preshene doted on me. She'd wash me in our little outside bathroom a few metres away from the house, bundle me up in a towel, surfer-board style, so my body would be suspended horizontally, and march back to the house. I would squeal with delight as the adrenaline flowed through me, the prospect of falling making me dizzy. As a teenager and young medical student, she got herself a holiday job, but instead of spoiling herself with the pretty things that young girls seemed to favour, despite her own shabby and sparse wardrobe,

Preshene would choose to buy me clothes. Just so her baby sister would have nice new things to wear..

I'm told it took a while for little Rita to warm up to me. For seven years she was the baby until I arrived and unceremoniously usurped that coveted spot, a wailing baby who interrupted her plans for play. Gentle, compassionate, soft-spoken Rita later became my crusader.

With the passing years the three of us became thick as thieves. Two older sisters meant I had best friends for life. Ours has been a love and a bond created from not having much but just each other. We have always had each other. And even through the material aspirations and successes in later life, nothing could break that bond. We are more than sisters, more than best friends. We are deeply and inextricably bonded. Where one's pain ends, the other begins. It is all the same, just split into three.

There is no trace of our tin house now. Across the road from where it stood though, there's the Shree Gengaiamman Temple, which is more than a hundred years old. It's a small, humble temple, and my great-grandfather Thambooran Gounden (a surname that later became Govender), who was among the first group of Indians to board a ship and sail to what was then called Natal to toil the sugar cane fields, was instrumental in its establishment.

The story goes that he spotted a growing anthill or mound, believed to be inhabited by the Hindu goddess Mariamman, who's also called the Mother. My great-grandfather marked the *puthu*, as it's known among the Hindu, as a sacred spot. Later, a wood and iron structure was built around the anthill, which eventually grew to touch the ceiling. Granny Allimah, or *aya*, as we grandkids called her, was its keeper for several decades before passing this honourable task onto Aunt Subbmah, my father's sister.

Devout worshippers came to cover the *puthu* in vibrant sari swathes to give thanks to the Mother for granting them their wishes. They kneeled before her with their hands drawn together in supplication: married women unable to bear children, young boys desperate for jobs, young girls desperate for marriage, the sick and the dying, prostrating to the giant mound of sand, beseeching Her to end their plight. As stories spread of the divine Mother's prowess to heal and make wishes come true, that small temple grew to attract thousands of worshippers.

As children, we danced around our *aya*'s worn-out sari in the hope of scoring some milk and fruit left behind by worshippers. Sometimes we were lucky and would get *jalebis*, that deathly sweet, bright orange fried Indian sweetmeat.

Now a heritage site, the Shree Gengaiamman Temple is the only remaining remnant of life before apartheid tore its way through our humble existence. As an adult, I have often gone back there to visit and pray. I stand at the steps of the temple, close my eyes, and sometimes if I manage to drown out the sound of the cars, I can almost hear my childhood somewhere out there. The laughter is trapped in a time gone by, before I knew of the insult 'Blackie' and before I learnt to fear a man's raised voice and hand. I remember that simple, happy life that was untainted. I have come to realise that sometimes in not having anything you have everything.

For me, this was the place of magic, where dreams grew like the anthill inside the temple, like the drums that heaved and sighed with boiling bath water atop a fire, like our tin house that expanded in the summers of our childhood. So too did our dreams for more, for a better life.

Born into poverty, my uneducated father worked relentlessly to give us a better life. As an adult I'd hear stories of how, on bitingly cold winter mornings, barefoot and wearing threadbare clothing, a young Frank Govender, on the threshold of adolescence, went out to the marketplace around what was then Warwick Avenue in Durban to help carry parcels laden with fresh vegetables and fruit for few pennies.

He became a waiter at the Blue Waters Hotel in Durban, then a bus driver and eventually a long-distance truck driver for Tanker Services.

He eventually moved us out of Cato Manor and into a little suburb in Chatsworth. It was there, from age five, that the neighbourhood boys tormented and teased me about my dark skin. A few years after we moved from Mayville, the extended family that remained behind were forcibly removed under the Group Areas Act, to make way for a sports ground.

My father never stopped working until I completed my journalism diploma at the ML Sultan Technikon in 1999. He was gone for a week or two at a time, transporting gas to as far afield as Botswana and Zimbabwe. His driving record was impeccable. Bone tired and hardly spending time with his family, he was always ready and willing to take on the next long-distance trip. No sooner had he walked through the door, he had to leave again. The time away from home and from us meant a few extra hundred rand, money we desperately needed to put me through Techikon, my sisters through medical school, and for feeding and clothing us.

Long-distance driving killed my father in the end. I was about eight years old when he was admitted to hospital for tuberculosis. He contracted it while out on one of his work trips. It took six months for him to recover, during which time he couldn't work. There was no salary. His colleagues collected money to help my mother put food on the table. It wasn't a lot, but at least we had food in our bellies. And we were better off than many others.

The charity of my father's work mates and even the neighbours who rallied around us during this time was testament to the man my father was. He was a noble man. As a child I was unable to appreciate that, but now it's the thing I boast about. I marvel at his selflessness and the sacrifices he made. Poverty never made Frank a victim. He did what he had to do for us.

He was never given any opportunities as a child or young man. My father's grandparents came from India to Durban to work as indentured labourers on the cane fields. They were uneducated and poor, and even as indentured labourers, their lives were apparently better than what they had in the dusty rural villages they came from in India. Their children and their grandchildren also struggled to make a living in South Africa.

None of them were educated, as an education was not high on the list of priorities. Finding a job and earning your keep was. At 12 my father was already contributing to his family's income. There was simply no time for an education.

Despite all of this, he gave us education, the greatest gift. At the time, it was certainly not a necessity for Indian girls. Within the Indian community, girl children were often seen as burdens, to be married off as soon as they were of age. Educating or empowering them was not seen to be of any financial benefit to the family. But my dear father was way ahead of his time. Marrying his girls off wasn't an option. He wanted us to be strong, independent and to have all the things he never did and could never give us. But he wanted us to have those things on our own strength and our own strength alone. 'You will study after high school,' he told us. 'You have no choice but to get a tertiary education.' But we could study whatever we wanted to.

Putting two kids through medical school and another through journalism school didn't come cheap, especially on a truck driver's salary. But he did it, by himself. He gave us education, so that we didn't have to be held back or down by the shackles of poverty. An education, he said, meant we would never have to be dependent. He repeated his mantra to the three of us: 'I don't want you to depend on any man for anything.'

My father may have been uneducated, but he was one of the smartest men I knew. My father ensured my sisters and I were empowered to be so much more than the great-grandchildren of slave workers.

I have the utmost respect for everything my father did for us. Yet our relationship was a complex one. For one thing, I often picked sides – my mother's, mostly – when she and my father argued. And they did, as all parents do. I resented him for upsetting my mother.

I remember being home from Johannesburg for a surprise visit during my time as an intern at the SABC. Some time during that visit my dad and mom got into a row. I yelled at him, saying I regretted coming home, that I didn't come all this way to listen to all their bickering. My outburst put a quick end to their argument. I spent the remainder of my time at home sulking and not really speaking to either of them, counting the hours to when I could head back to Johannesburg. As I packed my stuff into the car, my father sat outside smoking. We were about to hit the road, when he came to hug me. Almost sobbing, he whispered into my ear, 'I'm so sorry.' I never really accepted his apology. I held him half-heartedly, still angry about his and mom's argument.

I wish, how I wish I had held on a little longer and tighter. How I wish I had said 'It's okay, Dad, I love you.' But wishes are the longings of fools, forever trapped in a place of yearning.

I was often cold and distant towards him, and it never really eased or got better as the years passed. In punishing my father, I laid a rock-solid foundation for the bitter regret and remorse that would come to torment me years later and still does to this day.

Because I never got to make things right between us before he was taken away from us, much too soon. To this day it feels so unreal and so terrible. His death, on a rainy summer's night in December 2003, shattered my soul and ripped out my heart. It hit me with such force, my chest ached.

I walked into the cold and silent hospital ward where he lay in the middle of the room. The straight green line on a black monitor above his hospital bed was the first thing my eyes fell on. It was so final. It marked the end of my dad's life and the beginning of a painful undoing for me.

Who could have known a few days before, as he slowly made his way to the car to be taken to hospital for his next round of dialysis, that he would be leaving home, never to return again? The next time my father came home it was in a coffin.

My father had been condemned to a life of illness. He was poorly nourished as a child, and life as a long-distance truck driver was undoubtedly hard and took its toll on his body, which in the end failed his fighting spirit. He was young when he was diagnosed with diabetes. He'd had heart attacks and a couple of mild strokes. When his kidneys started acting up, he was sent for regular dialysis treatments. It was during one of these treatments that his organs began shutting down, one by one, and he was gone.

It marked the start of my self-imposed destruction. Because of my heartless, judgemental behaviour towards my father, after his passing I felt I had earned the right to destroy myself.

My eyes shifted to the still figure on the bed. He looked like he was sleeping. Like he had lived all his life, my father had opted to just quietly slip away. He waited for us to leave the hospital earlier that evening, when visiting hours were over. He waited patiently as we gently rubbed his forehead, whispered to him to come back to us. He lay there in a space and place beyond our reach; he waited for us to go.

The generosity of the Mother, whom my father and all of us prayed to at the giant anthill in the little green temple, had eventually run out.

When we left the hospital in the hours before he took his last breath, I had made a pact with whichever God was listening. I would do anything, just as long as he would be okay, so that I could make peace and tell him how sorry I was for not being a better daughter, and how thankful I was that he was my father. 'Just let him come out of this coma,' I prayed, 'and I will make amends. I'll tell him I'm sorry. I'll tell him I love him. I'll aim to do better and be a better daughter.' He never came out of the coma. And I never got to say any of those words.

I walked to his bed. His skin was already so cold to the touch. My sobs were unleashed: every sorrow that one soul could manage. In seconds the grief broke free, and to this day there's no sending it back or ignoring it. My cries cracked the stillness of that hospital ward. I leaned over and kissed his forehead and whispered in his ears the words he would never hear: 'Thank you, Daddy, thank you for everything.'

Just six months before, he had reached out to me, begging me to leave my boyfriend, my abuser. For my sake alone, he allowed the man who was hitting me into our home, and accepted his apology and a promise to do better, because I made it clear I wasn't going to leave that relationship. How I wish I had listened, held my father's hand and chosen to heed his plea instead of staying with the man who was beating me.

Every tear carried a lifetime of regret. He was beyond my reach now. The words that I promised to say if only his life could be spared rotted inside my head for years, constantly reminding me of what I allowed to happen by being cold and indifferent towards him for most of my life.

I didn't know how he felt, and not knowing and imagining what he *did* feel was devastating and debilitating. It was destructive, a constant shadow that gnawed at my mind and led my body to do irredeemable things to feel anything but that rawness of regret.

His body burning on the funeral pyre, clad in the one and only suit he ever owned, brought home the reality that he was gone, and I would spend the rest of my life longing for him, constantly living with regret and the words I should have said but never got the chance to. When death comes calling, you have no choice but to let it wrap its unseen arms around the person you love and whisk them away to a place and space that probably doesn't even exist, and in doing so, it turns the world of the living, the ones left behind, upside down and inside out.

The night he died we returned from the hospital, and Rita and I began the task of calling up relatives to tell them the news. It was 2am. People were asleep, lost in their dreams. My tongue felt thick and tired. With each call, I mechanically repeated the message I'd memorised as we went from A to Z in the family phone book.

And then, finally, I made the one call I didn't want to, wish I didn't have to. I called him, roused him from his sleep to tell him my dad was dead. He didn't deserve to share this moment with me. It should have been someone else, someone who had treated me better. But he was all I had, and he would have to do. Plus, I needed to get out of the house, even if for a few minutes. I needed to get away from sadness and the reality that was setting in.

When he offered to come over and fetch me, I quietly accepted. Hating myself on the one hand but, on the other, desperate to be anywhere but in that house. I needed a cigarette, to feel the silky sensation of the smoke enter my body and watch as the white clouds left me. I was pining for the catharsis my toxic habit would bring, stilling my thoughts and soothing the sorrow that had me in its clutches.

He picked me up and took me to a nearby garage. We sat in silence in his car as I drew on a cigarette. My eyes settled on the Chatsmed Hospital, where my father's cold and lifeless body now lay. I wondered if my dad's soul was around. Was his spirit somewhere in the air and space that surrounded me, watching me? Was my father also secretly aching to be with us, wishing he hadn't left?

He came to the funeral, with a bunch of my other Lotus FM colleagues. As my mother, sisters and I sat around my father's coffin, he offered them his condolences. Then he put his hands on my shoulders and asked if I was okay. My father was dead. It kept hitting me with renewed force. No, I wasn't fucking okay. I would never be okay. What a ridiculous question to ask.

But, I thought to myself, at least he made the effort to come to the funeral. He was always capable of these small saving graces, kind little things that would make me question if I was not too hard on him or too judgemental. Just as he was capable of being cruel, he could also be kind.

So many people came to say goodbye to my dad that day. It bucketed down with rain. The heavens were in mourning too, it seemed. I realised how little I knew about this man who lay in the coffin in front of me. People respected him. He had friends and family who loved him, people who were wreaked by sadness that he was no more. I found out more about the kind of man my father was the day he died. I found out more about him in death than I had ever known about him in all the days he had lived.

A week after the funeral that familiar old feeling of wanting out of life was creeping in. I didn't want to live, not when my father was dead. I was left behind, and I wasn't coping. My dreams were torturous. My father came back, and I would be holding him, hugging him tightly, telling him how sorry I was. It was good while I was floating there in the sanctuary of deep slumber, in that space where reality is unwelcome. But then I would wake up, disoriented, unsure of where I was. My own bedroom confused me – I would wake up still feeling drowsy, unsure of where I was, the walls around me making no sense. My own home had become a hell and then it would hit me: 'You stupid fool, he's dead.' And I wanted to be dead too. Breathing and living in an abyss of nothingness, I may as well have been.

One night, that voice that cajoled and coaxed me inside my head, begging me to end my life, found its way out. I told my mother I wanted to die, that I didn't want to live anymore. There, I'd said it. Those dark, secret thoughts that pervaded my senses came tumbling out of my mouth. My mother told me not to be silly.

I wondered if she knew that this was not the first time I wanted to end it all and that I was capable of actually doing it. I wondered whether she knew about the occassion when I had taken her sleeping pills.

We, each of us as close as we were – my sisters, my mother and I – suffered our grief alone. Grief is truly a private affair, even between those who share the closest bonds. We mourn differently. We regret different things. We are each trapped in our own little private hell. Grief made me want to die.

That feeling of wanting out of this life would always follow me. I realised that I could not deal with death. Abuse I could deal with. Death I couldn't. Abuse was easy to deal with compared to death.

Where was he in all of this? Going about his life. He called and SMSed regularly, but he was certainly not by my side. Other than at the funeral, I hardly saw him in the first few days after my father's death. It was his birthday five days after my father died, and he probably didn't want to be lumped with a grieving girlfriend, I thought. So, I should not have been surprised when he told me he would be going out with his brother and his brother's girlfriend – without me – to celebrate. But my heart broke a little. I don't know why. I should never have expected anything better from him. It seemed grief was a turn-off. I did not feel any compassion, patience or support from him during the most traumatic and lonely time of my life.

New Year's Eve 2004 came, and I remember thinking of him dancing and drinking the night away as I lay on the couch at home crying, wrapped so deeply in regret and remorse. I didn't want to go out, but I wanted him to be with me to see in 2004.

It was not a happy New Year's Eve for us. It signalled the start of a life without our father. When someone you love has died the world still goes on like nothing has happened, but your existence is altered forever. And you are forced to go on doing all the things you have been doing before death came calling, you are compelled to continue like nothing has changed when everything has. The world keeps on turning, unwilling to slow down, bend a little or give your grief some space, and you stay on it rotating through the routine of daily life. And for every single day that you are alive, your grief clings to you. It follows you and never lets you go. It becomes you. Your eyes will never quite look at things the same ever again. Who you were before death will never return. You will forget that person without even realising it. You morph into something unrecognisable.

I started drinking excessively in 2004. Every opportunity I got, I drank. I drank to drown out those feelings, to forget, even to remember. I just drank, always craving intoxication. It was a delicious sensation. The burn of the alcohol sliding down my throat, and that slow, seductive dizziness washing over me, numbing my body and brain. It was the ultimate elixir for grief.

I went out to breakfast with a friend one day and had three tequilas, enough to take me to that place where my brain was numb, and I could cry without caring about who was watching.

Brandy and Coke was the tonic for sorrow. I drank on an empty stomach to heighten the buzz. All I wanted to do was drink and cry till the saltwater in my eyes dried up and I could cry no more. No one in my family knew I was drinking so much.

I drank with him. He was a very willing drinking partner, and for that I was thankful. I was still the one who had to do the buying, as he could not be seen walking into a liquor store. I knew there was a chance I'd run into someone I knew but I didn't care. The allure of dizzy numbness that alcohol promised was far too great. I would risk being seen, I would risk the reprisal of my family and the Indian community for a quick escape into that oblivion that only alcohol can offer.

He and I would also often drink with the other Lotus FM DJs at Studio 13, the watering hole in the SABC's Durban office that was open every Friday afternoon. It was on one of these afternoons that his old habit returned. For a while after my father's death, the abuse stopped. I thrived in this fragile peace between us, seemingly brokered by death. But as afternoon turned into evening in Studio 13, our peace was broken.

He left to go to the men's room, and one of the other DJs started chatting to me. When he returned, he asked what we were talking about. 'Nothing much,' I answered. 'He was just making small talk. I wasn't even paying attention, to be honest.'

He was fuming. 'I will crack this bottle on your head,' he said, leaning forward and picking up a half-empty bottle of Jack Daniels. The tension between us must have been palpable. But the music was loud, so the others probably couldn't hear the heated exchange.

'Try it,' I challenged, emboldened by the booze. There were many people around, and I felt brave. He put the bottle down, grabbed me and kissed me hard, biting my lip and drawing a little blood. I got the feeling he did it deliberately to make a statement to the guys who were drinking there. Most of those present were men.

He had done something similar before when he once viciously bit my cheek, sucking on my skin. 'I'm going to mark you,' he said. 'People must know you belong to me.' I was left with a hickey on my cheek. Even with make-up it was very visible for what it was. I had to walk around at work with this garish and obscene thing. It was humiliating, to say the least. I was marked. He marked me. If any of the men were in any doubt, now they would know I was his.

It dawned on me in Studio 13 that day that the poison of the violence was back, insidiously snaking its way into our relationship again. But now it also became entangled with everything I felt after losing my father. I wondered one evening, after he had slapped me again in the SABC parking lot where we sat drinking, if my father saw that. The thought of my father being somewhere out there, watching the assault of his daughter made me desperately weepy.

All I could think of was the direction in which my life was heading. My father struggled to give me something better than what he was born into, and all of this was in vain, as I allowed another human being to degrade and damage me.

But given all the remorse I was feeling when I thought of my father, I also came to see the violence as punishment. I started thinking that I deserved it. I deserved every bit of it for hurting my father, for ignoring his pleas to end this toxic relationship.

The abuse felt like it was moving beyond threats, beatings and controlling behaviour to a level where there was just complete disregard for me, for my life. Our fights happened closer to my family home, where he promised my dying father he would never hurt me again, and he was becoming more callous.

One night after an argument I rushed to get out of his car as we sat parked in the driveway of my family home. My right foot was still inside the car when he threw it into reverse and backed out of the driveway. My foot got trapped in the door. I fell and was dragged behind the car, the tyre missing my face by inches. He said he thought I was completely out of the car. He didn't mean to do that. He said it was a mistake. He was sorry. I was lucky there was no serious damage other than wounded pride and scrapes to my scalp. Fortunately, I think no one saw what had happened, not even our notoriously nosey neighbour.

But I accepted my fate, I think because he was the one person who helped me escape the grief I still felt. We drank together, and then I could forget. And when I did remember, he was there to serve the punishment that I deserved. And ultimately, it was attention, acknowledgement and affection, from a man, during a time when I needed it most because my father was no longer there to give it to me.

Except his attention and affection was no longer with me, as he had moved on already. Tragedy and death sometimes draw people closer, binding them together and sealing their relationship. For us, tragedy did nothing. In fact, it tore us apart and drove him away. All of 2004 while I mourned, while I went through the lonely process of grief, he was busy building a relationship with someone else.

# EIGHT

# The Mother and the Wife in Waiting

One evening late in 2004, he and I were at Durban's famous Blue Lagoon having a drink when my phone rang. I didn't recognise the number. I answered and a soft, melodious voice spoke. No hello and she immediately asked to talk to him by name. Taken aback, I asked, 'Who is this?'

'His girlfriend,' she replied. I handed him the phone and told him flippantly his girlfriend was looking for him. I thought it was someone playing a prank.

He took the phone and said hello. Silence. Then he barked, 'Who the fuck are you? I don't know you, so please don't call me ever again.' He cut the call.

'Who was that?' I asked. No one. Just some girl trying to cause problems in his life, he said. I accepted his answer. I was a little tipsy. No threat to us he promised, dismissing her as nothing more than a troublemaker who was obsessed with him.

A few days later, I was getting dressed to go out with him when I got another call. I answered, and she told me her name. I recognised her voice. It was the same woman who called when we were at the Blue Lagoon. She asked about my relationship with him.

Still thinking this was someone 'trying to cause problems', I replied I was just with him for sex and money. That should shut her up, I thought smugly. 'Has he ever hit you?' she asked, a little breathless, a little desperate. Her question took my breath away.

'Nope. He has never laid a hand on me,' I lied smoothly, my heartbeat quickening. If she had been standing in front of me she would have immediately seen I was lying.

'He hit me, very badly,' she confided and went on to tell me they had gone to a local pool joint in Melville, Johannesburg, where she lived. He got horribly drunk and insisted on driving her car. She refused, and he beat her up quite badly for it.

I told her I was sorry to hear that, but he has and will never do such a thing to me. I'm not entirely sure why I lied. Perhaps I felt that telling the truth would mean I acknowledged their relationship.

She told me they had been dating for over a year. They met in India, where they were both holidaying at the time. He pursued her relentlessly while they were there. And when they returned to South Africa, he didn't stop and often went to visit her in Johannesburg.

Everything she told me made sense and seemed plausible – but I still refused to believe a word of it. I remembered his holiday to India with his brother and cousin. He called me almost every day just to say hello and that he missed me. When he got back he came to visit that same evening, a few hours after landing in Durban. The backseat of his car was filled with clothes and gifts he bought me in India. We sat there in the driveway of our family home and showed me each gift, one by one. He had impeccable taste and bought me such beautiful clothes. He had clearly been thinking of me while he was thousands of kilometres away.

How on earth could he have been having a whole other relationship when he and I were together pretty much all the time? How could he have been pursuing her while he was calling me every day from India to tell me how much he loved and missed me? It was me he loved so intensely that it drove him to rage. Me!

There were gaps, though, times when he was away in Johannesburg for work or some business scheme he said he was trying to set up, so he could quit Lotus FM, make some real money and marry me. But you don't see the evidence and question the things that don't add up. Because to do so could inflict a betrayal worse than being hit, worse than being insulted and demeaned.

How could I not believe her?

'You have my number,' she said. 'If you thought I were lying or making this up, you could block my number.'

'Speaking of numbers,' I said, 'how did you get my mine?'

She had seen all my SMSes on his phone. To cement her story, she mentioned the content of some of those messages. There was no way she was making it up. She must have seen them with her own eyes. She repeated playful messages sent during moments of happiness, messages dripping with ice and fury sent in moments of anger. Of course, I remember what I sent him. I listened in silence and disbelief, trying to come up with a valid explanation of how she could possibly know such intimate details of private messages that were meant for his eyes only.

That should have been another a-ha moment. It should have been. But I couldn't accept it. How could he have been having a whole other relationship all this time?

My mind was whirling, confused and dazed, but that small, feeble voice inside my head kept whispering it's all a lie. It must be a lie. He would tell me the truth. This was some jealous woman who was trying to break us up.

When she confronted him about me, she said he brushed me off as a psychotic colleague who was infatuated with him. No threat to their love or relationship, he promised. Well, that sounded painfully familiar.

With each passing second that phone call was like a revelation washing over me. My brain was in turmoil.

'Wait,' I said. Her first name triggered a memory. 'What's your surname?' I asked. When she told me, everything suddenly fell into place. A few months earlier I had found a printed email for an airline ticket from Johannesburg to Durban under the passenger seat of his car. There was a woman's name printed on it. Hot with anger and suspicion, I brandished the piece of paper in his face, asking him there and then whose plane ticket it was. We were in his car, on the way somewhere.

He was quick off the mark, I realised looking back, smart and cunning with his response. His brother had been using his car and he must have left it there. He didn't know who the woman was, probably one of his brother's girlfriends, he told me, never taking his eyes of the road as he spoke. Something niggled me about that story then, but I accepted it. How could I not?

And here she was, the woman whose name was on that piece of paper, talking to me on the other end of the line, confiding in me about my boyfriend, the 'delusional, fat, ugly chick', as he had described her after the call she made at Blue Lagoon.

I said nothing to indicate that I believed or trusted a word of what she told me. He was on his way to pick me up, I mentioned, hoping it would wind her.

This could be my opportunity to expose him for the fraud he was, I thought after that call. I could leave now and never look back. This was grounds for a break-up with no chance of reconciliation. He would have no choice but to admit to his infidelity. I was sure I'd caught him out, and my suspicions were validated. This time I would be the one to dish out the punishment. I could walk away.

But my anticipated triumph was short-lived. When he arrived to fetch me that evening, I told him about the call. There was no long silence, no stumbling and fumbling with words, nothing to indicate any dishonesty on his part. He responded immediately. She was a relative,

TOP LEFT: *Reporting from the scene for e-news Prime Time, 2011*

TOP RIGHT: *Ontlametse Palatse and I shortly after her very first television interview outside her home in 2010.*

BOTTOM: *When journalists let down their hair, 2009 – (from left to right) Marilyn Stanfield, Nicholas Jennings (eNCA producer) and reporters, Shahan Ramkissoon, Yolaan Begbie, me, Jody Jacobs and Dianne Hawker*

TOP LEFT: *With my soul sister Yolaan Begbie, 2008*

TOP RIGHT: *Celebrating Shahan Ramkissoon's birthday (far left) with Michelle Craig (middle)*

BOTTOM: *At a colleague's farewell in Johannesburg, 2009 – Yolaan Begbie, me, Shahan Ramkissoon, Michelle Craig*

TOP LEFT: *With Nikiwe Bikitsha at Yolaan Begbie's wedding in Franschoek, 2015*

TOP RIGHT: *Calling in to visit old friends at the eNCA newsroom in Hyde Park, 2017 – with Jody Jacobs*

BOTTOM: *Celebrating Michelle Craigs's wedding in Cape Town with the eNCA crew – (from far left) Iman Rappetti (former eNCA anchor) Yolaan Begbie, Serusha Govender, Shahan Ramkissoon and me.*

TOP: *With the maker of my dreams and my forever person, David, Kruger National Park, 2016*

RIGHT: *Making our wedding vows official, 47 years after my parents took theirs, 17 January 2012 (Courtesy of Chris Lynn Photography)*

OPPOSITE TOP: *Saying I do, 17 January 2012 (Courtesy of Chris Lynn Photography)*

OPPOSITE BOTTOM: *The happiest mother in the world – my best girl and I (Courtesy of Chris Lynn Photography)*

TOP: *Blessed to have a second set of parents – with my in-laws (Courtesy of Chris Lynn Photography)*

BOTTOM: *Wedding celebrations at Mitchell Park, Durban (Courtesy of Chris Lynn Photography)*

TOP: *Five pregnancy tests to be absolutely sure, the day I found out I was pregnant with my first child, 20 April 2012*

BOTTOM LEFT: *Preshene and I, 2015*

BOTTOM RIGHT: *Getting ready for my third baby, 2017*

TOP: *Diwali celebrations with Rita and Preshene, 2016*

BOTTOM: *Celebrating my 40th with my sisters and weeks away from giving birth to my last born, March 2017*

he told me, and was obsessed with him. She must have gone through his phone, which he left lying around, when she visited their home and seen my messages. That's how she knew I was his girlfriend, he explained.

'She is trying to break us up,' he said.

'And the plane ticket?' I asked.

He told me his brother used his car to fetch her from the airport, and she must have left the piece of paper behind. He didn't tell me this when I first confronted him about it because, he said, he felt I wouldn't believe him.

'Don't stress over her, baby, she is a fat, ugly fuck,' he repeated the offensive phrase. 'I love you.'

Once again, he so effortlessly conned and drew me back into his cesspit of deception and deranged love.

Six months after our final break-up, I found out they were getting married. During the phone call to me, she hinted that their relationship was heading in this direction. I chose to ignore it at the time, but when I found out about their impending wedding, I suddenly remembered the story she'd told me to illustrate how serious their relationship was by that time. He had taken her to their family flat on the beachfront to meet his mother, she said.

I worked out that it was around the same time that he must have taken me around to the beachfront flat, also to meet his mother.

The significance of this meeting was not lost on me. Like the woman who would become his wife, I knew meeting your boyfriend's mother was a good indication he was planning to marry you. In my case, a lot needed to happen before this moment came. I had to convert to his religion.

He had talked me into it. I had to change my faith for him and do it to keep the peace and show him I was loyal and committed to only him. I thought relinquishing Hinduism might be the one thing that could make him change. Maybe the beatings were all a test to see if I was really committed to him. I despised him, but I still wanted to hang onto the relationship. Without him I would be nothing. Like he told me over and over, no one would ever love me. No one could ever love me. And I could never do any better than him. I believed him.

I also felt I had to behave like a good Indian girl from a respectable family. He was my boyfriend. We had been together for a few years, and he was the first man I had intercourse with. So of course, I would have to marry him. There was no choice, no option – it just had to be. Otherwise, what would people say? What would people think?

I blindly agreed to convert in a futile attempt to make peace with and ensure the lasting devotion of a man simply because I lost my virginity to him. And so it came that I accepted his religion and tried to make it my own.

One afternoon, in front of the mother of one of my school friends who bore witness to my conversion, I washed my hands, feet and face and, with both hands cupped, recited a few words. In uttering those words, I renounced Hinduism and accepted a faith I struggled to make sense of, especially since the person I was doing it for broke so many of its rules.

The rules, I found out during some of the classes I attended in preparation, included always washing your hair after having sex, and abstaining from sex when I had my period. I was taught how to fast and pray. Pork was a no-go. That was hard. I remember the smell of it sizzling in a pan, making me feel hungry and long for my previous life. But I didn't give in to the temptation.

I wore the long, flowing dress, but I always felt like an utter and complete fraud in the wide expanses of its shapeless folds. It was every bit as restrictive as it was loose. It hid all my curves and contours, so the sight of my body would not arouse any man.

There were about five or six of us in the conversion class, all women, and most of us did it for love. We knew our relationships would and could not go any further until we had become something other than what we were born into.

Everything I was raised to believe became a thing of shame and a thing to be rebuked. I had to choose a new name. I went for an exotic Persian name, just because I liked the sound of it, but I battled to bring it over my lips. I later looked up its meaning, and it is associated with a need for freedom, both physical and spiritual, and its keeper is someone who wants to make a difference in the world. The irony was not lost on me.

Baptised with the new name, I ripped off the red string that had adorned my right wrist forever and renounced Lakshmi, the beloved goddess of fortune and prosperity, and Hinduism. I gave up the colour and vibrancy of my culture and a faith as old as time for a religion that I felt dictated and defined who and what I should be as a woman. The man I was with certainly did. I had to be taught how to be better at the new religion I had adopted. My mother was horrified. But she knew better than to try and dissuade me.

And so, it was that, a few months after this monumental, life-changing event, I found myself sitting across from his mother at the beachfront flat. I was wearing a long skirt and my hair was covered in an attempt to look respectable and like I had been born into their faith, like I had been living their way all my life.

Her words to me that day I will never forget. She sat there, stiffly and unfriendly, regal in traditional religious garb. She wore her contempt of and for me proudly.

'Go where you are wanted and where you will be loved. If my son ever married you, it would be a huge embarrassment to our family,' she said, her voice dripping with ice, unfeeling and unforgiving.

'Why?' I asked, when I knew very well. I opened my eyes widely as I had read somewhere that it's a way to prevent tears. I had to do all I could not to break down and cry in front of her.

I was dark skinned, and my family didn't have the kind of money his family did. Being dark skinned was worse than not having money. Once again, my coffee-coloured skin had become my curse. Another human being had succeeded in making me feel so utterly ugly and pathetic – all because of my skin colour.

When I later realised she must have met the woman he ended up marrying around the same time she met me, I wondered why his mother kept that to herself. It was abundantly clear she didn't approve of me, partly because of my looks, and his future wife was everything but the 'ugly, fat fuck' he had made her out to be. I saw them together once after we had split – and she's really beautiful.

Were his mother smart, she could have told me he was set to marry someone else, a woman who would not embarrass the family, and without much effort, she could have put an end to our relationship in their family flat that day. Had she just told me, she could have had her heart's wish come true and seen the back of me. Why would she keep quiet? How could she aid and abet his dishonesty? Why she didn't, I would never know or understand. Why his mother kept his infidelity a secret has baffled me ever since. Maybe it was her way of being kind, not wanting to be the one to break my heart.

Or maybe she was protecting her son. But either way, she ended up being the perfect excuse I needed to end our relationship once and for all.

# NINE

# Picking Up the Pieces

The days and weeks after I walked away from him were hard. I'd tried to walk away countless other times during our relationship, but I always went back. Always enticed by promises of doing better, charmed by words of love and soothed by apologies. A pretty little trinket or perfume won me over.

I also kept going back because I didn't want to be alone. I didn't know how to be on my own. I believed I would be alone because he made it clear that no man would and could ever love me the way he did. And if I ever thought about having a relationship with someone else, I would be ruining *their* life. What do you mean by that, I asked him once.

'Simple,' he said. He would make that person's life a living hell. He would, he said, make them regret ever laying eyes on me. He smiled and kissed me gently on the lips. 'So don't do that, don't go and ruin someone else's life,' he said.

Fear kept me bound and shackled to him. I was so afraid. After all, I knew first-hand how dangerous he could be. So, I would leave, and he would talk me into coming back. On and on it went during the years we were together.

But when I walked away that last time in 2005, something had shifted inside my head, my brain and in my soul. I saw myself with new eyes.

There were still moments of weakness, when solitude and being away from him would become more a misery than a luxury. I may have just started a new job and enjoying the thrills of being on TV, but as much as I was surrounded by people, everyone wanting a piece of me, life was lonely. It was a desperately dismal thing that I could share with no one.

I felt alone and frustrated. I had sudden bouts of longing. I second-guessed myself. Did I do the right thing by walking away? Part of me wanted him back, while the other part knew that it was a terrible idea because he would continue to destroy me. I chastised myself for wanting him back.

I also had this sense of giving every ounce of myself to another human being and not having a single thing to show for it. The scars and gifts don't count. I had nothing tangible to show for all the effort I had put in and everything I had been through. In a sense, it felt like a waste.

When I heard he was getting married, I was crushed. It had only been six months since our break-up – so much for being in love with me.

I sent him an SMS, one loaded with sarcasm, congratulating him. I couldn't help myself. Hidden in that message though was a plea for reassurance that he did love me and that this marriage was some horrible joke.

And he obliged. His reply made my heart sink and almost sapped away all my resolve to live without him and be free of the depraved bond we had. He thanked me and said he was being forced into this marriage. It was me he loved, he wrote, and he would always love me. I managed to stay strong and not fall for the deceit.

A couple of months after getting married, he contacted me again and persisted with the story; he wasn't in love with her and was having a secret affair with me in his head. He even once invited me along to

Dubai for the Bollywood film awards. 'Why don't you take your wife?' was my cutting response.

These messages messed with my head. Just when I started being okay, getting comfortable with being alone, and finding an inchoate sense of strength, just when I could smile again and really feel a sense of peace, a text message would come and undo everything and send me careening back into that space of uncertainty and anxiety.

Time passed. Days went by. I lived between the high of my job, the seduction of fame, and the almighty downs of being the one who, despite having walked away, was the one who was left behind. Perhaps that's why so many women end up back in the arms of their abusers – you are plagued by thoughts of the terribleness of being alone.

When you have been drained of all self-confidence, you find yourself desperately seeking out the source of the drain because only that source holds the power to make you feel like you belong and give your otherwise meaningless life some meaning.

As I tried to piece together my life without him, I got a call from a woman. She said she was his mother-in-law. She demanded to know the nature of my relationship with him. I told her we had broken up but that he was still pursuing me and sending me messages about getting back together. 'I have all his messages on my phone,' I told her, 'and you're welcome to see for yourself.'

I didn't want anyone thinking I was still hankering after him or trying to ruin his marriage and weasel my way back into his life. She wanted to see for herself if what I was saying was true. We agreed to meet. I wanted him exposed for what he was.

But he found out about the meeting. He called me, sounding frantic and desperate, pleading with me not to ruin the 'one good thing in his life'.

'Are you kidding me?' I shouted. 'You and I both know what you have been trying to do, so go to hell and don't call me again.' I slammed the phone down. I was struggling to breathe. I was a braver person than I was when we were together. I felt the power that comes from emancipation, from walking away. I might have been weak and distraught in those first days and weeks after the break-up, but I could feel myself growing stronger and braver. It's what happens when you decide to break free.

A few hours after we spoke my mother called me. I knew something was wrong the moment I answered. 'What have you done?' she asked me before I could barely get a hello out.

'What do you mean?' I asked. A little chill crept up my body even though it was hot outside.

'What have you been doing with him? He called me now to say you're trying to break up his marriage and that he has naked photos of you and he's going to put them on the internet.'

I was stunned. I was expecting trouble, but this? My mind reeled. Naked photos – what the hell? I was in a tailspin. I could certainly not recall posing for any photos. I was struck with fear – naked photos all over the internet would ruin my reputation, just as I broke into television reporting. But more than the fear of my professional reputation being at stake was the cold realisation that his call had revealed to my mother that the two of us had been intimate.

Many in the Indian community see sex before marriage as a disgrace. Young girls who are sexually active before getting married are deemed to be 'spoiled'. And I know my mother well enough to know she'd be livid and disappointed. One day when I was around 13 I was helping her in the vegetable garden. Bent over sowing seeds in the soil and planting caution in my head, my mother delivered the talk about the birds and the bees. 'Wait till you're married,' she instructed. 'Make a good name for yourself.' It was the same thing her mother had told her, and she was proud of honouring this wish. My father was the only man she had ever been with, she told me.

I had let Mom down. All her talks of waiting for marriage and not letting the family down had fallen on deaf ears the first time I had been intimate with him. And now she knew. I felt betrayed that he had outed me like that and ashamed that I had deceived and betrayed my mother. But I was not surprised. He was twisted and devious when we were together, so why wouldn't he be when were not?

But my mother surprised me. 'You should have confided in me,' she said. 'I will always stand by you, but you need to tell me what's going on in your life.' I wasn't expecting this answer. My usually prim and proper mother wasn't judging me or admonishing me. She was comforting and consoling me.

I started crying, unable to even begin to comprehend the strength and love she showed me with just those few words. She wasn't going to shun me or turn her back on me. She was offering me her unconditional love without judgement and reserve. It was more than I deserved, I felt.

I told her I never allowed him to take pictures of me. Surely he was lying. Unless he had taken photos of me while I was sleeping. There would have been plenty of opportunity. We used to go to a dumpy little flat his family owned where we would drink, watch movies and finally fall into a boozy sleep as the *azaan*, the call to prayer, sounded from the mosque nearby.

But would he stoop that low? I still wanted to believe that he wouldn't do that to me and harm me in this way, despite all the things he had done to me before.

I asked her what she said to him.

'I told him to stay away from you,' she said, 'and that if he ever tries to cause trouble in your life, we won't let him get away with it. Everyone will know what a first-class rubbish he is.'

I had to stifle a laugh at the last bit, but I had to hand it to her – she was no pushover Indian mom. She could hold her own. After all the lectures about living a 'decent' life – implying no sex before marriage – she put aside her beliefs and rules to offer me support.

She also told me she called his mother. Their home number was still saved in our phone book. 'Why did you do that?' I asked, exasperated and feeling quite exhausted by all this drama. He was out of my life, had been out of my life by my own choice and doing – and suddenly here he was again, still very much part of it. Tainting it with his toxicity.

'No, I'm not letting that piece of shit hurt you ever again. His mother must know what a rubbish he is. His parents must control him. We don't want to know anything about him. He must leave you alone. Last time we let him get away.' She ranted on.

'So, what did his mother say?' I was curious. I wasn't going to pretend otherwise. 'She just kept quiet and listened. Then she said she doesn't know what this child is up to and why he's doing this. She said she'll tell his father and they will talk to him.'

It was one thing talking to my mother over the phone, but that evening I had to face her. I knew she supported me, but regardless, I was still really embarrassed by the revelations of the day. My mother gathered me into her arms. For a long time, she just held me without saying a word. Eventually she broke her silence: 'You made a mistake. I will never judge you for it.'

That was all she said. It was all she needed to say to make me weep. I wept for the wasted years, for choosing him over my family when they begged me to leave him. I wept for my father who – thankfully – wasn't around to know that I had betrayed him and my mom with such careless abandon for my chastity. I also wept for the fact that he was still trying to destroy my life without even being in it. Did he ever really love me?

Nothing ever came of the threat to release those pictures.

A few days later, his wife called and asked me if I honestly thought he was going to take me to Dubai.

'I am pretty sure if I had said yes and packed my bags I would have been on the flight with him to Dubai,' I hit back.

'He was only trying to make you feel good about yourself,' she laughed. She sounded smug and went on to tell me how many times he said he'd cheated on me. To cut me down to size? Or maybe she was hoping to make herself feel better now that she knew she was married to a philanderer. He'd also confessed to messing around with one of his co-hosts on Lotus FM while we were together, confirming the suspicions I had back then. The two of them used to laugh behind my back, his wife told me. She seemed to take pleasure from delivering each blow of betrayal. He and I were long over, but that didn't mean it didn't cut to my core to hear about all his infidelities.

I should have ended the call. But I hung on and listened. Which is a good thing, I suppose, because his wife's final revelation to me made me realise how I was taking my life into my hands by sleeping with him. She told me that before they got married, she asked him to take an HIV test.

In that moment, I realised, more than his words and fists could ever hurt me, he might have put my life in danger every time we were intimate. And I was oblivious, blindly trusting and believing when he said he had never had sex with anyone else. 'It was negative,' she said.

I only plucked up the courage to take an HIV test two years later. It was World AIDS Day, and I was one of the e.tv reporters who agreed to take the test live on air. I had always been terrified of needles, but I realised, more than that, I was secretly petrified of being positive. I was acutely aware of how reckless I'd been during our time together.

A good few million people watched as the nurse pricked my finger and walked off set with the sample to get it tested. I took an HIV test live on national TV to help give others the courage to find out their own status, and I knew just how easily my result could have been positive.

It felt like I'd been holding my breath all the while waiting, and when the result came back negative, I jumped for joy. I felt lighter, like I could breathe again. I rushed out to the deck at work and lit a cigarette, pulling the smoke in as far down into my body as I possibly could.

I realised I was angry for what he had put me through, that he was so callous about my life and my safety. He lied over and over about me being his first and only lover. I was angry for having believed something so utterly ludicrous. I was angry with myself most of all.

But I was young, vulnerable and desperately seeking love, and I was willing to cast aside all logic and rational thought. I trusted and believed anything that fed my self-esteem and made me feel remotely special.

I still recall how dry my mouth was when I took that test and how fast my heart was beating. I knew I had gambled with my own life every single time I was intimate with him, always ignoring my gut, which kept on telling me that he was not doing this with just me. I never listened. Listening to my gut would have meant acknowledging what a fool I was. Whereas heeding it would have spared me a great deal of pain, both physical and emotional.

The test was necessary to remind me how high the stakes really were.

## TEN

# *Lights, Camera, Action!*

Durban was becoming small and claustrophobic. It was 2008, three years after the break-up. You can walk away from an abusive relationship, but it follows you wherever you go and in whatever you do. It's always there – a constant reminder – and when you're the one alone, it's even worse.

My job at e.tv was going exceptionally well. I had won two awards. In 2006 I was named KwaZulu-Natal Vodacom Television Journalist of the Year for a story I did on the death of dozens of babies at the Mahatma Gandhi Hospital due to a klebsiella outbreak. Our cameras captured the unbridled grief of dozens of mothers, many of them first-time moms. The second award came in 2008 for a story on a new-born baby who was thrown into a pit toilet and miraculously survived.

I became widely recognised. Wherever I went people would stare or stop to talk to me or ask for a photo. Many people told me I was 'flying the flag' for the Indian community. They were so proud of me and thrilled to see an Indian woman on TV. I would take the compliments with as much humility as I could. I often thought back, though, to growing up in an Indian community and being ostracised for my looks, specifically my skin colour. I loved and hated the admiration.

But it was thrilling, such a high, unlike anything I had ever experienced. A car guard shouted my name across a busy parking lot, and I saw people from all races – white, black, Indian and coloured – recognising me. I thrived on it. I greedily gulped every bit of attention I got. It fuelled my self-esteem and fed my ego.

For so long, I had been starved of praise and being made to feel worthy, and I shamelessly revelled in the fame. There were times I couldn't quite believe the turn my life had taken. Everyone, even the bully boys of my childhood, suddenly wanted to know me, claiming to be close friends with me, proudly saying they once went to school with me.

Vanessa Govender was suddenly everyone's champion. I could live with that.

But he was also always there beside me and inside my head reminding me never to forget that no man would ever want or love me like he did. But after gaining fame, I had men eating out of my hand. I still considered myself ordinary, nothing special, but the ugly truth of my past combined with fame and attention was in a way turning me into what he was: greedy for attention, hungry for that feeling that comes from knowing people want to know and be with you. I left a trail of broken hearts. I knew I could have my pick of pretty much any man I wanted.

I had hit rock-bottom, lost my father and my boyfriend, which was traumatic, regardless of the fact that he was an abuser. He left me hardened and unrepentant in love, and the never-ending grief following the death of my father crushed me and wore me out. We're, all of us, the end product of all our experiences, and I am no exception.

I looked everywhere for validation and to steal energy from other people. I looked for love but never quite found it during this time. I dated and then stopped taking calls or refused to see these men again. Some of them were desperate to get to know and understand me other than as 'the girl from TV'.

I dated some of the most handsome men: talented actors, good men, successful guys who were always doing their best to win my heart and affection. But I never hung around too long. I couldn't. If I didn't feel the butterflies and the connection, I didn't stay. Being with him taught me never to settle or compromise. I knew what I was looking for in a partner.

He ended up being wrong; many men loved me, but I was in control now, determining how much affection or attention to give. I could be compassionate and then savage in the next instant. I used the admiration from men to satiate my hunger for feeling wanted, needed, beautiful and untainted. I used them to build myself up and gather all the shattered bits. I used them to try and mend myself. I fed off the lust in their eyes and the love in their words. But none of them could ever get close enough to know and understand me. I kept them at a distance. Cruel, is how one suitor once described me. And perhaps he was right. Because after what I had been through, why wouldn't I be cruel, hard and forever suspicious of anyone and everyone?

I was also determined that no one was ever going to get the better of me again. My fame contributed here; it made me feel indestructible, unconquerable and powerful beyond measure. But inside, in the deepest part of me, when I was alone with myself, I knew I was nothing more than a tainted, frightened, lost person with nothing to really offer anyone.

On the upside, because of being bereaved, I became a more sympathetic listener, I think, and in this way also a better storyteller. But rather than feel-good stories with happy endings, I found myself constantly seeking out tragedy. The big stories of the day are hardly ever good news ones, so that also contributed, but there was something in me then that was drawn to the sorrow of others. I think I might have been looking for kindred souls so that I did not have to feel alone in that god-awful place that I was thrown into the day my dad died.

I still cringed every time I had to say my father was dead, that I didn't have a father. I felt ashamed to say it. Because I felt like he chose to leave me when he died. He chose to go away and leave me fatherless. And as much as I grieved, I also felt angry and cheated. That he abandoned me and never gave me the chance to tell him I loved him. I caught myself thinking that my father *forced* me to seek out sadness and death.

Death and grief followed me everywhere. I wanted to believe that people drowning in their anguish opened up to me and shared their stories with me for the country to see only because they recognised a similar torment in my eyes and aura. We always found each other: a mother in a township whose children were hacked to death by their own father, or a wealthy dad who killed his disabled son and wife before trying to take his own life.

I think I needed them more than they needed me. With each tragic story I covered, I became more lugubrious. But I couldn't stop. It was a drug that fed my soul. As a journalist I became the buffer between victim and viewer. I absorbed their pain and anguish. I was right there in the middle of the grief and suffering. I took it in and felt it intensely. The stories I ended up telling could often not even begin to relay the impact they had on me. The stories stayed with me long after they'd been written and I'd gone home. I was so intimately connected to the anguish of the people whose stories I told, there was simply no telling where my grief ended and theirs began. It slowly eroded my soul, until one day I found myself falling apart at the seams.

Fortunately I realised that something had to give, and I thought perhaps a change of scenery would do the trick. There were too many ghosts for me in Durban anyway, and he was still there too, which meant there was always the chance we could run into each other. I don't know what I dreaded more, running into him and his wife or him alone, which would be the perfect chance for him to try and lure me back into his arms. And I wasn't sure I'd necessarily be able to resist. I was weak, but I was also strong enough to know this weakness about myself.

I thought that to the people who knew we were together, I seemed like the one who got left behind, because I was still alone, when the truth is I was the one who walked away. But in walking away, I also got left behind. A clean slate would be a good thing, I thought.

I asked for a transfer to Johannesburg, and in June 2008 I made the big move. I was to be part of e.tv's new 24-hour news channel, and I anticipated how my fame would multiply, my name would be spoken on many more lips and my face seen by many more eyes.

Leaving Durban was an attempt to put distance between my past and my present. I needed space from my mother too. I had to learn to live without her, so that when the time came I would already know how to go on without her. I was, I think in some way, preparing for her death by getting as far away as I could from home and from her.

Johannesburg opened her arms to me. Another small-town girl searching for something elusive – peace, love and excitement in a city on steroids. I loved that it was so cosmopolitan. I was finally in a place where I came into my own.

But the first few months were awful. I was terribly homesick. And the Johannesburg newsroom wasn't for sissies. I had to work twice as hard to prove myself. I got the feeling my shyness was sometimes taken as arrogance and that some of my colleagues felt that I thought too much of myself. But they might not have suspected how delicate the ties were that held me together. I felt like I would never be able to love, let alone like what I saw in the mirror. But Johannesburg and being able to spread my wings soon fixed that.

I worked hard and gave every inch of myself to every story I covered. I was still drawn to stories of human suffering, no doubt trying to heal myself and still my own pain by looking long and hard into the sorrow of others. Then early in 2010, five years after my father died, one such sad story marked the beginning of my healing path. I heard about little Ashleigh Louw, a girl who was born with a rare medical condition where the heart grows outside of the chest cavity. I was assigned to find out more. I remember walking into Chris Hani neo-natal intensive care unit and seeing this tiny birdlike creature inside an incubator strapped to so many cords and wires. There it was – her little heart pumping away furiously on her chest. The moment my eyes fell on her, I knew Ashleigh was going to have a monumental impact on me. She was destined to be part of my journey.

Ashleigh was a fragile little thing who was defying death with each breath she took. And she stirred up all these emotions in me. I envied her a little; she was slowly dying, and I still went on living, waking up each morning despite the desire not to.

In our newsroom I became the go-to reporter on Ashleigh's condition. And I was wearing the darkness of that terribly sad story; it shrouded me. Everything around me was closing in. There were times I couldn't breathe, it got so bad. I was drenched in sadness.

During this time, dreams about my father became more frequent and would leave me completely gutted. I woke up in my little bedroom in Fourways completely disoriented. In all those dreams, my father came back, and I held him and talked to him. Those dreams had all the moments I wish I had had when he was alive. They were beautiful, but they destroyed me.

I always wanted to sleep. I waited for nightfall, so I could lay my head down and slip away to a place out of reality's reach where my father and I were united. I rose every morning still feeling desperately tired and wanting to go back to sleep, mostly so I could be with him again.

I wasn't coping, not with my own grief, which seemed to be multiplying over time, and not with the stories I'd been covering. The distance between home and Joburg didn't empower me or give me greater strength to take on the world. No, it was destroying me. I felt I needed to go back to Durban.

In a meeting with my editor, Patrick Conroy, where we were supposed to discuss this option, everything that had been kept hidden and secret for so many years just came pouring out. I was feeling suicidal, I told him, and I knew that this time around the feeling was different. I was alone in a new city away from home and I was very afraid of and for myself.

I found an unlikely confidant in Patrick that day. I always felt Patrick didn't like me too much and that he was hard and unrelenting when it came to what I did on air, but I was wrong about him on so many levels. I saw it in his eyes that day: understanding and empathy. For the first time in my life I was telling my own story, and someone was not just hearing it but listening to my every word.

He understood in an instant, I think, how my work had become entangled in my personal life and how there was no beginning to one or end to the other. It was destroying me. 'Not every story is about your father,' one of the news anchors said to me before, but it was only during this chat with Patrick that that penny started dropping.

I needed to see a counsellor, Patrick said, and e.tv provided one. I refused. It was enough to talk to him; I wasn't going to sit on a chair and do the clichéd nonsense of talking to a shrink. I certainly wasn't going to regurgitate my sorry story to someone else.

He pulled me off the Ashleigh story. I was shattered. So, I made the appointment with the counsellor. I had ulterior motives; I thought if I went to see her, then Patrick would have no choice but to put me back onto the Ashleigh story. I didn't plan on saying much to the counsellor. I was too tired to talk anymore.

The next morning I walked into the counsellor's office and began to speak into the silence that surrounded us. I was restrained at first, but then, for the second time in that week, my physical self had no control over my mouth or mind, as every bit of pent-up pain found its way out. I gently laid it out before the counsellor; it was never-ending. I sobbed as I recalled a lifetime of torment. Every incident, every word fired at me, every bit of hurt came hurtling to the surface, finding its way out of my memory onto my tongue and out of my mouth. And there was a whoosh of relief to be finally let out.

I can't even begin to describe the release. The heavy thing that resided in my chest had been lifted. I wasn't carrying this by myself anymore.

It was probably the best thing I'd been forced into. I felt more seen, more heard. I felt cleaner and lighter than ever. When I was done I was so spent that I felt physically drained and sleepy. That night I slept like the dead. I struggled to wake the following morning. I hadn't had that kind of deep, peaceful sleep for a very long time.

As I made my way up to the newsroom the morning after the session with the counsellor, I got a call to say they were stopping Ashleigh's medical treatment; death was hours away. I told Patrick I needed to go back to the story because I also needed closure. I threw my visit with the counsellor in as a trump card. Despite my expectations of a fight, he agreed and I was back on the story.

I sat on the bed in my flat and watched her take her last breath in her mother's arms. It was the first and last time that Anastacia Louw, Ashleigh's mom, would ever hold her child. Ashleigh's aunt sent me the video. I listened as the heart monitor beeped, one last beep, saw Ashleigh's heart stop, and heard Anastacia's soft, strangled cry, a single sound shattering the silence of the hospital ward. Seeing the straight line on the monitor threw me back to the night my father died. I wasn't seeing Ashleigh anymore; I was seeing my father's lifeless body.

If it weren't for that meeting and Patrick's ultimatum, I can't say where and when it would have all come to an end. Because it felt like it was coming to an end for me. I was tired of waking up every day and walking around with the things I carried inside my head and of seeing other people suffer. I was just tired of everything. Despite the adrenaline of television and the newsroom, the high of fame, the many people surrounding me, and the partying, life was lonely. It was nothing more than a game of charades, where I pretended to be something I wasn't. The flirt, the clown, the mystery, the sex bomb, the snob, the ice princess – I was all this and more to different people, but I don't think anyone ever knew who I really was. I didn't even know who I was. Everyone knew my name, but it felt like none of them knew me.

The counsellor recommended that I be transferred back to Durban to be closer to my family and have their support. Patrick told me the good news. I could go back home, try it out for a month or two, and if I was happy I could stay or come back when I felt strong enough.

But the interesting thing was, I was already feeling strong enough to stay. Because a short while before I was given the all clear to go back to Durban, another young girl crossed my path who inspired me no end – another story that became a marker on my road to healing.

When I met her, Ontlametse Phalatse was much older than her 13 years of age. She was suffering from a very rare genetic disorder called progeria, which made her body age too fast. She was an old woman trapped inside the mind and heart of a teenage girl. At the time she was the only known black child in the country – and perhaps the world – with progeria. And that was the angle and selling point I used to convince my assignments editor that it's a story worth covering.

Even though I was prepared for what she'd look like, she still took my breath away when she walked into the kitchen of their modest little home in Soshanguve, north of Pretoria. She was the size of an eight-year-old. I hugged her and her bones felt so fragile, like I could crush her without even trying. But what she lacked in size, she made up for in spirit.

She was so tiny that I had to kneel to hold the microphone to her mouth during our interview. As I listened to her, something broke inside me, and I couldn't control the tears that fell freely and unashamedly down my face. This child must have thought me such an odd adult, crying for no apparent reason.

It is strange how those of us who have no desire to live are the ones who have no choice but to carry on living while the ones who are desperate to stay alive are the ones who are dying through no choice of their own.

Ontlametse made an impact on me in ways that words are simply inadequate to capture. I was mesmerised by her grit and strength, her optimism and charm. Simple, untainted and just there. And there I was, more than twice her age, and I felt like I was falling apart at the seams. My illness was not as transparent as hers, but it was just as debilitating.

I clung to her every word, breathed in her childlike determination and savoured the taste of her optimism. I tried to ingest every bit of the power she was exuding from her tiny body. I wanted to make it my own. She was everything I wanted to be, so I told her story with as much purity and poignancy as I could. Ontlametse embodied everything I wished I could be. I thought to myself, if a spunky, ancient, 13-year-old can grab life by the horns and swing it around with glee, what was the excuse of this 33-year-old?

So, I remained in Johannesburg. I felt beautiful in this city. And I knew I needed never fear running into him here; it was way too big for that to happen. My father continued to haunt my dreams. He was never dead, and I was always getting to hold him. My dreams took my deepest desires and turned them into short little films made in slumber.

I was learning to live and to carry on, because that's what the world forces you to do. It goes on like nothing's happened, even though everything has happened to you. You have no choice but to stay stuck on this spinning planet, biding your time and doing your thing until you simply don't have to anymore.

I had stopped searching for love, even though I never stopped craving it. I wanted children, but I felt it was never going to happen. I also thought about that almighty kick to the stomach and wondered if that might not have damaged something inside me and ruined my chances of falling pregnant.

In my own community, I was considered way past my sell-by date for marriage and a family as I was in my 30s. And after the abuse and the bullying I endured as a child, I didn't think I was able to be in a relationship with an Indian man again. I dated only white men. And I resigned myself to dating but never committing. I thought I was never going to be stuck with a man and, more importantly, that no one was going to claim ownership of me again.

# ELEVEN

# *Kismet*

It was 2011, and I had just turned 34. The small town of Ficksburg in the Free State was on fire as violent service delivery protests erupted on its streets.

At the forefront was a young father, Andries Tatane. He later became the symbol of service-delivery protests across South Africa. We all watched, transfixed, as the police beat him in full view of television cameras. And as the violent confrontation between police and protestors raged in the background, he took his last breath on the streets of Ficksburg and became a casualty of the ongoing battle between government and the people.

I was assigned to cover Andries Tatane's funeral. Ficksburg was cold and dismal the day he was laid to rest. I stood shivering in the icy cold, filing continuous updates from the funeral. The hours dragged by. I was tired but flying high off the adrenaline of television, and as a stranger I witnessed a family's saddest, most private moment. I secretly shared their pain because I understood and knew what lay ahead of them. I drank in the sorrow, stored it in my head and made it my own.

That evening I went back to my flat. After sharing a flat in Fourways initially when I first moved to Johannesburg, I had struck out on my own and rented a flat in Northcliff. It was cold. I took a hot shower and washed away the emotions of the day; they stuck to my clothes and skin. I reeked of death and sorrow. I let the hot water wash away all the smells and traces of the grief I had witnessed hours before as Andries Tatane's coffin was lowered into the ground and his widow watched and wailed. By the time I got home, the story had already been airing on e.tv's 24-hour news channel, and it later led the prime-time news bulletin. Millions would watch it.

No sooner had my story aired than I heard a 'ping' from my phone. Someone had sent me a tweet. I carried on watching the news, thinking I'd check my phone when I went to bed. It would give me something to pass the time and hopefully lull me to sleep.

Someone, a man by the name of David, tweeted me to say how moved he was by my Tatane story and how angry it had made him. I never responded to viewers and wasn't planning to do so now. I mean what was I going to say? I didn't think it needed a response.

Perhaps it was something about the gentle sincerity in his blue eyes in his Twitter profile photo that compelled me to tweet David back. There were a few more tweets between us that evening and in the days to come we cautiously exchanged phone numbers.

We slowly got to know each other. David told me he lived in Durban and owned a bakery. I knew the place – my sister bought us treats from there when she started working as a doctor. Baked goods were a luxury we could never afford when we just lived off my father's salary.

The bakery was also a stone's throw from the Durban e.tv office, and it was a place the camera guys loved to stop to grab breakfast or lunch on the way to or back from covering a story.

To think we'd been in such close proximity to each other for so many years and had never – not once – knowingly run into each other. But now we were 600 kilometres apart and we had discovered each other. It was kismet.

He told me he saw me reporting from Johannesburg and was a little sad to see that I had moved from Durban. 'Was it because of heartbreak?' he asked. I was taken aback that a stranger could see through me without even knowing the first thing about me. 'Partly,' I replied and told him a watered-down version of that part of the story.

David and I continued to talk every day. SMSes evolved to phone calls. He asked permission first, and when the phone rang and his name flashed across the screen for the first time, my heart started beating so fast. When I heard his voice for the first time, waves of heat cascaded from my head to my feet. I felt something strange and new, not unpleasant and certainly welcome. David thrilled me. The thought and prospect of David thrilled me.

But he was still a viewer, and I remained overly cautious. I only revealed the bits that I thought were palatable, that wouldn't crush the image I thought he held of me.

He said the first time he saw me on the news he felt sorry for me, but also couldn't help having a good laugh at my expense. It was one of the first stories I did after joining e.tv. It was a piece on hair trends, and I interviewed a top Durban hairdresser. As part of the story, I was treated to a special hair makeover on camera. I wasn't told what was planned and I had no say in it either. When it was all done and my swivel chair was swung around to face the mirror, the largest bouffant hair in the world surrounded my face. I almost fell off my seat! I could see the cameraman's body convulsing with laughter as he hid behind the viewfinder of his camera. But I couldn't let the temperamental hair maestro know how utterly mortified I was. I did my best to hide my embarrassment and tried to deliver my piece to the camera with sincerity.

I could not get out of that salon fast enough. And as soon as I was out of sight, I gathered up my teased and tortured hair and tied it up. There was no way I was going to be seen in public with that crazy hairdo. And as soon as he was out of earshot the cameraman roared with laughter. Neither of us dared offend the hairdresser from hell.

David told me what a good chuckle he had seeing me with that appalling hairdo. He said he even felt a little embarrassed on my behalf. It was also the moment, he said, he fell in love with me.

# TWELVE

# *Let's End at the Beginning*

Several months passed before David and I plucked up the courage to meet face to face. I walked through the airport terminal in Durban and there he stood, half hidden by the crowd. Everyone there was waiting for someone. And there he was, someone waiting for me. We had been waiting for each other pretty much all our adult lives without even knowing that we were.

The hustle and bustle of the airport arrivals seemed to dissipate into the background when my eyes first fell on him. Before that day, all I had were a few photographs he sent me on the phone, and they weren't the greatest. They certainly didn't do the man standing before me any justice at all. It was always his eyes that drew me to him. They were gentle, calm, compassionate and passionate. Those eyes spoke a story without the man needing to say a word. I knew I would never get tired of looking into those eyes and that even when old age and sickness would inevitably come, I knew I would remain in love with those beautiful blue eyes.

The moment we saw each other, I knew this man. I'd known David all my life. It was the feeling of familiarity and peace that could only come when you're with someone who lets you soar, who elevates you and keeps you grounded all at the same time.

We lived in Durban, and somehow even in that close proximity of where we lived and worked, we'd never crossed paths. All the times I'd visited his little bakery, we'd never run into each other. But there we were, strangers meeting for the first time, and in an instant, we knew each other. We had known each other without ever having met before.

Long before, in moments of loneliness I had made a mental list of the traits of the man I would love and wanted to love. I made a mental list and implored the universe to find him for me.

I knew I would and could never marry an Indian man. Not after my abusive relationship, and certainly not after the prejudices that I'd faced in my own community. I also didn't think I had the emotional strength to deal with rejection from an Indian mother because of the colour of my skin.

The white men I dated seemed to like what they saw. For them, there was no, 'Even though you're dark, you're pretty.' I was pretty because I was dark skinned, sexy because of my dark skin. Yes, those white men taught me not to just like myself but to *love* the skin I was born in.

Once I left Durban, I discovered that I was beautiful and that the sin of my skin in my community was the thing of immeasurable appeal elsewhere. What a liberating feeling to finally be able to look at myself and not despise what I saw.

And David, he made me feel like a goddess. In his eyes I could see the beauty of myself. In his words I could see the value of my life. In his life I came to finally revel in my own.

For David, our fate was pre-ordained. It was written in the stars, our particles destined to gravitate towards each other through the centuries and through time. He told me he had loved me for a thousand years, and I laughed and told him that's some line.

At first, even as the relationship grew, I never allowed myself to expect more from him. I refused to believe he was in love with me or could love me with absolute sincerity or purity. But when he asked me to marry him, I knew and finally understood the truth of his words. I understood the promises in his kiss, and I felt alive and beautiful under his gaze and touch.

Where one mother once told me, it would be a huge embarrassment if her son ever married me and one man punched me and called me an ugly black bitch, another mother and her son from another race group showed me so much kindness, love and acceptance that it healed the scars left by my own people.

David and I got married in January 2012. It was a sunny morning, and in a gazebo in Durban's Mitchell Park, he and I promised to love and honour each other. A few close family members gathered to share our special day.

To honour my dad, I chose the day to coincide with what would have been my parents' 47th wedding anniversary. He couldn't be there to see me get married, but I would keep him beside me in this way. I was always looking for ways to keep him alive and present.

I cried on the morning of my wedding for all the things he had missed in my life and because he would never know I was safe at last and had found happiness and love. I cried because, as happy as I was, I had never let go of my dad and still yearned for him.

During the ceremony, out of the corner of my eye, I spotted him in the distance in his favourite cream and blue cardigan. He was standing under a tall tree, his hands in his pockets. In the still summer air, cigarette smoke drifted through the space that divided us and ignited a memory so forceful I had to take a deep breath not to throw my hands to my face and weep. I saw him watching from afar for a little while. Then I got distracted, and when I looked again, he had softly disappeared. What I would not have given to whisper in his ear, 'I'm safe, Dad.'

Once considered a crime, mixed marriages and families embody all that is beautiful and possible for South Africa, and while we should never forget, we should also be slow to fuel the fires of racism by painting everyone with the same brush. That's what my interracial marriage and love has taught me. That's what it has opened my eyes to.

Four months after getting married, I quit my television job. It wasn't an easy decision. Relinquishing my passion and fame for a quiet life was always going to come with a little bit of regret. Coming back down, slipping into that place of just being ordinary was never going to be easy. But television had done its work for me. It was time to let it go and start a new journey.

I was ready to start a family, and I needed to do it without carrying the trauma and grief of others. I needed to cleanse myself of the emotional anguish that journalism had bequeathed on me, so that I could be a good, sane mother.

I didn't know it at the time, but when I handed in my resignation letter, a new life was already growing inside me. I did my last story on television, cleaned out my desk and left that world of grief, sorrow and fame behind as I headed to our beachfront flat in Durban to get supper ready for my husband and plan for the future. I got into my car and headed off to the beginning of a new life, a new journey.

We were keen to start a family, but we were unsure how long it would take. And I still wondered if I would be able to fall pregnant. I was 35 years old, and I was still unsure if the kick I took to the stomach had not perhaps left me unable to bear children. All these thoughts were running riot in my head.

To celebrate my early retirement from journalism and television, David took me away for a weekend. I had big plans, wine under the stars, just the two of us, talking about our life ahead and trying to have a baby. It was going to be a party, just the two of us.

David suspected something was up though and just before we left town, he asked me to take a pregnancy test. I'd wolfed down my breakfast that morning. I was craving a boerewors roll – and it hit the spot. I woke up feeling famished, which was unusual, as I could go a whole day without eating.

I laughed uncontrollably. 'Don't be daft,' I said to him. 'I would know if I were pregnant.' Just take one, he cajoled, to be on the safe side. 'You don't want to be drinking if you're pregnant.'

So, we bought a test and headed off. We stopped at a petrol station, and I ran off to take the test. When the two lines appeared, I thought that meant I'm not pregnant. I'd read the instructions carefully before taking the test, but somehow, I think my brain refused to accept that after more than a decade of waiting for love and wanting to be a mother, it had finally happened.

I waved the test in front of David's face, laughing with glee and an I-told-you-so look. I saw the initial uncertainty leaving his face. His blue eyes were dancing with excitement.

'Darling,' he said, 'you're pregnant.'

'What? Don't be absurd,' I responded but suddenly felt unsure about what the two pink lines actually meant.

I was pregnant, four weeks already, which I confirmed as soon as we got back from our weekend away.

I cried. I sobbed my heart out as we got back into the car and headed off to the game reserve. I was pregnant. There was a baby growing inside me. I cried uncontrollably.

Because in that moment all I could wish for and think of was my father. He would never see or hold my child. And more than anything in the world I desperately wanted to be able to call up my mother – and father – in that instant and say guess what? I'm having a baby. But that was never going to happen. I would never be able to speak to my father. He would never know his youngest child was having a baby.

My tummy, which once took a kick from a tan Caterpillar boot, was now home to a life. My body, which was once beaten and worn out from being alive, was carrying two heartbeats. It was all too much to comprehend.

My son was born before the year was out. And I missed my father even more the day he came into the world. I felt a stab of jealousy and insurmountable sadness as I watched David's dad proudly hold his grandson in his arms a few hours after he was born.

Two years later our daughter came into the world, and I began writing this book, as she lay nestled safely within my womb. For the sake of my children my secret needed to be told. If I were to love them without reserve I had to expose the torment that had ruled my life for so long. I had to let it out and let it go, and in releasing it replace it with love for my children. There was not enough space or place for me to harbour resentment and love at the same time. There was not enough space to hold onto the past and be in the present.

This book, this story was to be my letting go. But in starting it I was dredging up all the darkness again, and as I sat typing away feverishly recalling the pain, reliving it even, I would feel my daughter stir inside me, almost like those dark thoughts and memories were finding its way into her safe space. So I stopped. Because that darkness would follow me from my recollections into my reality; I would become moody and despondent. All these years later it still had such a powerful hold on me. The atmosphere in my home would shift from peaceful camaraderie and happiness to grim silence. It was sapping me of energy and destroying me bit by bit. I stopped writing, but I never forgot about the blank pages begging to be filled.

Late in 2016 I discovered I was pregnant with my third child. I was lying on a couch in a cold hospital ward as my sick son lay sleeping in the bed next to me. Earlier that day David said I should take a pregnancy test, and I laughed like I did the first time. He has always been more in tune with my body and my soul than me. I bought a test from the hospital pharmacy. At 3am I went to the loo and took the test out of boredom. Two pink lines emerged; our third child was on the way.

I could barely believe my luck. To think I once doubted if I could even bear children. I honoured my father by giving this new baby his name. And as I sat waiting for my son to wake up, I decided to honour and celebrate my children by finishing this story and closing this chapter of my life once and for all.

For the third time my once-abused body was proving its resilience and its beauty by doing something so miraculous. For the third time my body showed me it had forgiven me for all the trauma and pain I had put it through. Because it was forgiveness in its highest and purest form when every single time that place deep inside my belly cradled and grew a life. It was forgiveness for the brutal kick and for the countless slaps and punches. It was my body saying it was healed. My mind, though, remains a different story.

But human beings are truly amazing. Through the decades and through the centuries there are people who show the world what human beings are capable of. They teach the rest of us that there's a fire that burns deep inside, a hunger and a desire that knows no name, that has no definition, but all it ever wants is to survive in the hope of experiencing something better the next day.

Throughout my third pregnancy I continued writing this story. Some days I could do it without holding back, and other days I had to relinquish it for the sake of my sanity.

Our third child was born in 2017.

While our youngest will never know her grandfather, she will have him with her all the days of her life. Wherever I go and whatever I do I always try to keep him with me. Because that's all death leaves you with, the need to grasp at things that will allow you to hold on and never let go. With the passing years I have struggled to hold on, as he has painfully slipped out of my grasp. The weights that hold the memories down have become weak. There's nothing you can do as they slip out of your grasp and you watch them disappear. Time vanquishes the intensity of memories.

I am loved and I am safe. I have all but forgotten what it's like to be afraid, to live in constant fear every time a voice or hand is suddenly raised. I can't identify with that kind of fear anymore, so much so that I sometimes wonder if I dreamt it all.

I look at my children and I marvel at where I've come from and where I am. Poverty, bullying, demeaned because of skin colour, abuse, grief, sorrow … all the things that broke me down bit by bit over the years have slowly and painstakingly been mended by the love of my racially mixed family.

In my world, where I was once shunned and discriminated against by some of my own people, I found tolerance and peace with a white man. I can never go back and give that little girl who cried as she was taunted and teased all the way home from school any comfort or tell her she was beautiful just the way she was. I can never go back in time and mend her wounded spirit and heart. I can do nothing for that child.

Just as I can do nothing for that young woman who got slapped, kicked and beaten up almost on a weekly basis.

My children will never know the heartache that comes with being born dark skinned, but being racially mixed, they will undoubtedly have their own battles to fight.

That's okay, because in our house we teach tolerance and love for everything and everyone. We teach a young boy to respect his sisters and mother, and to always treat them with gentle kindness. We teach our little girls not to be princesses but warriors. We teach them that every shade of every human being is beautiful, and our skin colour – whatever it may be – is what makes us so special.

I'll never tolerate my son toying with a girl's emotions or treating her badly. I'll never tolerate the things my ex's mother tolerated, condoned and protected, because I want to raise a good, noble and strong man, a man with honour and integrity. I want to raise a boy who'll grow to add value to the lives of the people around him and never rob anyone of their self-esteem and worth.

That would be my gift to my son and my daughters, so that they may never do to another what was done to me and never have to put up with what I did.

In our home we don't talk about race because we have shown its irrelevance.

David gathered up all my shattered pieces and helped me put them back together. This man with his gentle blue eyes, who encourages and motivates me to be a better person and makes me want to wake up and live every day, has made me forget needing and wanting to die.

This book has, in some ways, never been about the abuse and about my abuser. It has also been a love story. A love story of my journey of finding myself that has waited patiently to unfurl and blossom, as both David and I trekked through life, taking its cruel twists and mind-numbing turns, as we gravitated towards that one moment when our lives and worlds would collide and become one.

They say everything happens for a reason. I can't find a reason why anyone would want to physically abuse or emotionally destroy another human being. I can't figure out the reason for my abusive relationship.

But I do know the reason I survived it. I know the reasons why, even after swallowing sleeping pills, I woke up and continued to wake up despite desperately wanting never to.

I lived to nurture my body – which stood unyielding despite the barrage of punches, kicks and slaps – so it could create something profoundly beautiful. Three times over. Those three little lives taking their turns to grow deep inside me, healing and showing me there has always been a greater purpose for me. Showing me that even in the darkest places, life survives, and it can thrive. That the human spirit, in spite of insurmountable grief and sorrow, knows nothing else but how to survive and go on.

But it can only do this if given the chance. I had wasted so many chances over the years, believing myself to be unworthy, incapable and powerless. I never was. Believing something doesn't make it a reality or true. Once those beliefs were replaced by new ones – that I deserve better, that I am capable, that I am the only one who has ever been in control even in those moments where things around me weren't – only then did I have the courage to do the things that I feared.

The feeling of absolute power that came from taking control of my life surpassed the high of TV. I'm not brave. I have never been brave. I just simply chose to take control. I wanted more for myself than just being a victim.

In fact, I've never been a victim. I have always simply been a survivor. We all are. The things we experience, the pain we endure, the heartache, the sorrow, the grief, the humiliation – all of it doesn't make us victims. Not for as long as you draw breath, for as long you wake up every morning to do it all over again and for as long as you never stop wanting something better for yourself, you're never a victim. You're a survivor, simply surviving. And for as long you remember that you have choices – whether it's to stay or walk away, whether it's to love again or whether it's to quit a bad habit – you're powerful beyond measure. Even in grief there's a choice: submit or embrace it and own it, take it with you wherever you are, never let it go, but allow yourself to smile, even laugh, throughout. And one day you'll find that you can actually feel the laughter and the smiles reach right into your core, that you can feel happiness, contentment and even peace. You can feel it so intensely and profoundly that it's no longer a charade just to make others feel comfortable around your sadness. You feel it without having to feel guilty about the dead or the ones that hurt you.

That's the human spirit that can never be extinguished; that's the human spirit that will never break.

Ask the mother who'll never hold her child again or see that child grow, dreams and hopes scattered in the wind into nothingness. Ask that mother who still wakes up every day and goes on despite her insurmountable sorrow. Ask her why and ask her how.

Ask the little boy living in the informal settlement who knows nothing but poverty, who goes to bed hungry, filled with longing for a life better than what he was born into. Who still wakes up every day and goes to school and never stops dreaming. Ask him why and ask him how.

Ask the drug addict who, despite coming from a wealthy and affluent family, has made the streets his home. Who throws pride away and begs at traffic lights to buy his next fix. Who tells himself tomorrow he will stop. Tomorrow he will clean up his act. Ask him why and ask him how.

Ask the woman who has been punched, slapped and kicked who stays with her abuser believing he will stop, he will change. Ask the woman with the defeated soul who never stops hoping, who never stops wanting something better, something other than the hell she's in. Ask her why and ask her how.

Just ask me, and I'll tell you. Because we always have choices, and for as long as we want something better, something more than where we're seemingly trapped, in those places and spaces of sadness and hopelessness, we have choices. We always have choices. The choice to go on, or the choice to languish where you are. The choice to choose differently, make a change, accept what you've been given and change what you've been given. The choice to give up and the choice to rise above. Life is filled with choices. And therein lies unimaginable potential to soar or to sink. Choice is power, and many of us fail to realise that each of us, despite our circumstances, are powerful beyond measure.

Because even when you're beaten, you can choose not to be broken.

# Epilogue

*6 August 2018*

I am tired. I haven't been sleeping well for a few weeks now. For a couple of months, a few select people have been privy to my most private thoughts, my brutal words and the terrible things written about in this book. The prospect of strangers now pouring through the most traumatic time in my life petrifies me.

Some nights I sleep like I am dead to the world. Others I lie awake into the early hours of the morning, the world asleep, but with me lying on my bed, my head spinning, feeling sad and afraid. My every nerve alert, my every pore triggered. I stifle the sobs that sometimes threaten to rip open my chest. I feel like I could flood this world with my tears and my sadness. I feel like I am drowning in it myself some days.

It has all come back with a vengeance. Everything that was done to me has come back. Writing this memoir – going over each incident over and over, finding the words to express what happened and what I felt at the time, needing to read and re-read and then trudge through them again and again – has triggered every dormant demon that has been biding its time in the deepest part of me, waiting to be acknowledged. Waiting to be mourned. Waiting to be healed.

I should have known a wound left untreated is bound to have devastating consequences. I have filled my life and world with things and people over the years so that there is simply no room for any part of my past life in me. And every time a memory of that time would try sneak its way into my present, I would stand a little taller, laugh a little louder and live with little more vigour to dispel that despicable image and leave it sulking and skulking in the furthermost corners of my brain.

I am counting down the days to the book being on the shelves. There is no excitement. No thrill. Nothing. Just a heightened anxiety brooding within me. Trepidation. I have good moments. I have great moments. I talk to myself, reason with myself. In a breath its gone. Some days I want to become air and dust. Some days I have a cyclone raging inside my head and a tsunami building beneath my skin. I am angry. I am furious that I never stood up for myself back then.

Emotions waxing and waning from second to minute. Me in the middle.

The trauma of an event can make you travel to places and it can deceive you into thinking you have it under control. As I near the end of putting this memoir together, it has made me feel like I am disconnected from myself and from this world.

Hold me tight – I silently send a prayer into the universe that it may be delivered to my loved ones. Hold onto me. As overwhelming as these feelings are to me and as painful as they are for the people who love me to see me like this, they are necessary to my healing. I have to feel it. I must feel it. And from it I will emerge a little spent and a little scarred, but I will come out of it. Of that I have no doubt. You see I didn't start this book, I didn't start this journey to just crumble into a helpless heap and become a victim all over again.

Let me feel this raw emotion. Allow me to wallow in it for a bit. Only just for a bit. I have earned this. My body and my brain deserve to have a moment or two. Because I don't want to be stuck here for too long. I have far better things to do.

I am more than the slaps and kicks and punches. I am defined by a simple fact; I am here. I am here. Still standing.

All my past has ever wanted or needed was to be acknowledged and mourned. I did neither up until now. I have resurrected the darkest, most traumatic days of my life and I am finally grieving for the girl I used to be. That girl has been desperate for the woman I am today to acknowledge the pain and the trauma she went through all those years.

But there is a bigger picture. I have placed myself at the altar of sacrifice of what people may say and think just to alter the way we treat this evil that permeates our homes and communities. A story to imbue others and a story to heal myself at last.

Regret, regret, no time for you now. There is a war to be won.

Fight or flight? I am choosing to fight. I am choosing to own my fears and my sorrow, to fight and find my way back to myself.

I was a girl on the threshold of life when I almost had the life snuffed out of me. I am a woman now, I have laid myself bare and shared all my secrets. There is nothing left to know, there is nothing left to diminish me with.

With every slap, every punch, every kick, this book was delivered to me. There are good days, there are great days and there are days that pass by in a blur. But I tell myself, that's okay.

I am chaos and peace. I am happiness and sorrow. I am clawing my way out and I am trying to slip away. I am here and I am nowhere. I am so many things all at the same time. Every second I morph, I shift inside myself and in the spaces, I inhabit.

I am sometimes desolate, but I am always determined. I am always determined. Through the ups and downs through the despair, I am always determined.

I understand that I need to own my grief and my fear because without it I would be failing myself all over again.

Measured and meaningful talks with oneself is necessary. Reminders, the kind things we would say to someone else in a similar situation, we must also reserve for ourselves. We deserve our own kindness and empathy before we can even think about dishing it out to someone else.

I have started therapy. Thirteen years after waking up face down in the car park of the SABC office in Durban, I have begun the process of fixing myself on the inside. There is no shame. I honestly do not feel shame for anything I have shared with you.

Fear yes, sadness yes. Shame, definitely not.

Who would have ever thought that speaking and owning the truth could be both liberating and so debilitating.

One day at a time…

# Acknowledgements

Behind every story ever written is a battalion who stood steadfast and encouraged the dream, who gave of themselves and their time to help that story unfold, whether on the pages of a book or in the days of the life of the author.

Behind my story are some exceptional human beings who gently held my hand and walked me to safety. And then there are those who read the initial drafts recounting those dark painful days.

I am the great-granddaughter of immigrant number 77530. My grandfather was a gardener, and it seems my father was never destined for anything more than menial work in his lifetime. He was shackled by a system designed to keep him uneducated and living in poverty and dictated to by the archaic rules of a community in which girl children are expected to be subservient, unimportant and often uneducated. But Frank Goonabalan Govender was never going to let his girls slip into obscurity. He gave me the gift of an education.

Dear Dad, I have been searching for you constantly since the day you left. Words lie rotting inside my head never to be spoken or heard. Your gift, your selflessness has given me the power to do this, to gather my memories and turn them into words in a book for all eternity. It will be your legacy long after I am gone, long after all memories and traces of you and I have diminished, even in the minds of those who will come after us. This book will remain. Our story will stay long after we are gone.

I wish that you could know I am safe and loved. I wish you could know that I eventually found courage, even when I really was living on nothing more but reserves. Thank you, Dad, for believing in us and for having the wisdom to see and steer beyond the confines of the times. I have always loved you even though I may not have known it in my times of obstinate rebellion against you. You remain one of the greatest men I will ever know and love. This book is my gift to you wherever you may be floating among the stars, drifting in spaces of nothingness. You are not forgotten. And I will never stop trying to find you.

My sisters, Rita and Preshene, thank you for never turning your back on me even when I chose the side of my tormentor. Neither of you relinquished me. I can never forget the fierceness with which each of you fought to try and get me out of the cesspit I was stuck in while gently giving me space to come to the realisation of its toxicity by myself. This could not have been an easy read for either of you. Our father never meant for us to be ordinary, and I hope we have made him proud. Thank you for loving me and continuing to mother me even at 40. You are both remarkable women and will always remain at the forefront of my legion of supporters.

Dearest Mom, where to start? You defied all the conservative norms when it came to me, the rebel. You packed away your manual on raising a good Indian girl and instead gave me room to discover, empower and eventually emancipate myself. You stood by me when I would have really expected you to shun me. I can just imagine your fear and worry every time I got into that car and went off. I am a mother now, and I shudder to think what you had to endure every time I left the house. Forgive me, Mom, for the poor choices and near fatal decisions I made.

I get you now. I get you. You are the epitome of resilience and fortitude. You are no pushover Indian mother, that's for sure. You have made your mistakes, and you allowed me to make mine, and after it all went out with the tide, you gathered me in your arms and held me. How can I ever thank you?

My daughters are richer for having the blood of you three remarkable women flow through them.

To the friends who never left even when there was no reason to stay. Former Lotus FM presenter Aasra Bramdeo, the only person who had the courage to confront me with her suspicions, who listened and advised when most others pretended not to even notice the bruises, scars and the defeated spirit diminishing me with each passing day.

Years have passed since those dark days at Lotus FM, Aasra, but you didn't even need time to think about whether you wanted to get involved when I asked if you would back me up. You spoke of things I didn't even remember. I shuddered and I wept reading through your recollections. Once again you reached out to help me, lifted me up and gave me courage. Thank you.

Dr Nadine Rapiti – you made me your business. You took the time and you made me your business. Thank you for caring enough and reaching out to me. It's people like you who are the saviours of people like me.

Dearest Thabiso Sithole, in turning my back on you, I surely didn't deserve your absolute kindness and compassion when I contacted you all these years later. Your memories of me and that time broke my heart into a million pieces. Forgive me, for I was a different person. We were soul mates, you and I, clicking instantly. I am sorry for what you have to read in this book and even sorrier that I never stood up for you. All things fade, some things leave me, but your friendship and you never did.

Dr Rajendran Govender, Uveka Rangappa, Shahan Ramkissoon and Sibusiso Miya, thank you all for also remembering and writing down your own recollections of the girl I once was. All of you expressed the regret of never having done more to help me get out. Please know this, I understand the profound difficulty that you face when you are confronted by the abuse of another human being. We are scared and reluctant for fear of ruining relationships and even causing further trauma in the life of the victim. It is okay. In agreeing to recall and give me your written statements, you have helped me more than you can imagine. Thank you for doing it and for not saying you needed to think about it. Each of you immediately said yes, and I hope you realise that any regrets you may have had for the past were erased the second you agreed to help me. I appreciate what you have done.

My army is big and strong. When I began writing this memoir a few years ago, I had only three chapters, and I was wracked by uncertainty. I wondered: Do I continue? Is there anything of value in the story of my life? I sent those first three chapters to my former e.tv colleague and friend Joanne Joseph.

'Tell me,' I asked her 'if there is potential in this.' Joanne was the very first person to lay eyes on my words and to know intimate details of what happened to me. Dearest Joanne, your advice guided me to write with more feeling and compassion for myself, and in doing so a few years later, those three chapters morphed into more, and here we are now. My heart-felt gratitude to you, Joanne.

Few things are more powerful than women who stand in the background behind others, who nurture and encourage their sisters, so that they can shine while never even seeking a moment's glory for it. Yolaan Begbie Aguemon, my soul sister, you are one of these women. You gently nudged me and fed the dream.

'Read this,' I said 'and tell me if you want to know more.' Your answer brought me here, thousands of words later. I have told the world everything. Thank you, my poppy. You know I have tons of love for you. I feel lighter and I feel more liberated.

'The best place to hide is in the light.' That is what Debora Patta, former editor-in-chief at e.tv said to me when I expressed my fear of laying myself bare for my community and country to see. Thank you, Debora, for instantly agreeing to add your name to my story, for your kind words and encouragement. You chose to stand with me and hold my hand and make me even stronger. Thank you for that phone call in 2005. I can't even begin to explain what it did for me. It filled the cracks of what came from years of emotional taunts that ravaged my self-worth and confidence. You inspired me to want more for myself. I remain yours faithfully.

Patrick Conroy, my former editor at e.tv, you forced me to seek help at a time when I ran out of reserves, to wake up and breathe. In that moment when I let my anguish spill out, I saw in your eyes such immense kindness and empathy, and it made my falling apart all that much easier. I reached out to you in a time of absolute desperation, you grasped my hand and helped me to save myself. Thank you, Patrick. You're a wonderful soul.

No one person can get to where they are going without the help of others. Charlotte Kilbane, Franci Henny, Nina Callaghan and Andy Duffy, you raised me up, so that I could bask in the limelight. Thank you for contributing to my television career. Because of each of you, I could shine. Thank you for playing an absolutely crucial role in my big journey of self-discovery and worth. You guys were the dream team creating television magic and ensuring us reporters lived the motto of 'No Fear and No Favour'.

To all the super-talented camera crew at e.tv who were always happy to indulge my crazy ideas: together we pushed boundaries and created truly great television. I shone because of each of you. Terence Stone, Meshack Dube, Joe Komane, Tewis Brink, Xolani Cele, Dave Coles, Linge Ndabambi, Sbu Miya, the late Dotcom, and my favourite guy, Dan Mafokoane. 'Make me look beautiful,' I would say. And the response was always, 'We can only work with what we have.' I have so much love and respect for you.

My story could have just stayed stuck as words on a computer, never to be seen, read and known by anyone besides a select few of my closest friends. But Nadia Goetham, my publisher, brought me out of hiding. She is another in my army of women. Nadia, you allowed me to share my secrets. Even as you battled your grief and sadness, you took on mine, so that we could share it with the world. You have given me the platform to speak out and own this dreadful thing that has happened to me. You have gifted me with an arsenal of words to highlight the rot and evil that permeates our homes, our communities and our country. Thank you is insufficient. I appreciate you, my dearest Nadia.

Also the other exceptional women at Jacana Media: Bridget Impey, Lara Jacob, Tarryn Talbot, Neilwe Mashigo and the rest of the remarkable marketing team, I am because of you. Thank you so much for all the hard work that you all put into bringing this book to the shelves..

The real magic and hardest part of putting memoirs together is not so much the remembering and writing down, it is the cleaning up of words strung together, of sentences woven together, to make it poignant and powerful. My editor, Joey Kok, you too took on my ugliest memories. You graciously and patiently trudged through it all and gave the world this book back. Thank you for unjumbling my words and thoughts. Yours was not an easy task.

Angels on earth do exist. Emma Sadleir of the Digital Law Company, I breathe a little easier knowing I have someone like you on my side. I am deeply indebted.

My beautiful saviour, my sanctuary, my person, David ... you painstakingly helped mend all my broken bits, you healed my shattered soul and made me whole again. You listened as I poured out my past, and you quietly fixed me with your love, gentleness, kindness and strength. I have been elevated. I am soaring. You are the maker of my dreams and have lit the fire that burns within me. From the word go, you encouraged me to write, to get it all out. You made sure of my healing.

When the invite came to pitch my story to the publishers, I turned it down, petrified to leave an eight-week-old baby behind, but even more scared to pursue this dream. You told me to change my mind. What if they say it's too late, I lamented. 'Trust me,' you said. And I did. And here I am, my love, trying to express my gratitude and love and coming up short. I will always come up short, because, you see, words are never going to be enough or adequate, nor can they capture the depth and breadth of this fire between us, this chemistry that's defied race and religion. I am safe because of you. I am loved because of you. Where some would have seen someone spent and wasted, you saw my potential, and every single day you imbue me to do better and be better and happy. Even when I feel like I am slipping away, out of my own skin and out of this world, as I sometimes do – such is the eternal curse of what I carry – you hold on so tight. You keep me grounded, you encapsulate me while never stifling or suffocating me. You keep me here. You keep working so hard to keep me happy. I am not easy to love or hold sometimes, I know, but you do such a sterling job of making my world and my life something I want to be in. I love you, David.

And to you, dear reader, thank you for taking my hand and stepping into the pages of this memoir, into the dark memories that I once guarded so fiercely. By reading my truth, you have each taken a tiny piece of the burden that has weighed me down for over a decade. You have helped me in my healing and you have empowered yourself to hopefully never stand back and shrink into the shadows when confronted with abuse, whether it's someone you know or your own. Thank you.

As you read these last words know that somewhere right now, a woman is looking into the eyes of her partner and taking her last breath. Perhaps shot, perhaps strangled, perhaps beaten, she is dying. She will never get to hold her children or see them grow, she will never graduate or know the thrill of truly being in love and being loved. She will never get to sit at the feet of her father or mother and pour out her past. She will never become a mother herself.

Take a breath, dear reader, take a deep, long breath and savour its beauty and the profound joy it brings, because somewhere in this instant, there is a woman who will never again be able to take one.